# Is There Life After Death?

*A Novel View*

# IS THERE LIFE AFTER DEATH?

*A Novel View*

by

SJOERD L. BONTING

www.whitecrowbooks.com

For information, contact White Crow Books
at P. O. Box 1013 Guildford, GU1 9EJ United Kingdom,
or e-mail to info@whitecrowbooks.com.

Cover Designed by Butterflyeffect
Interior production by essentialworks.co.uk
Interior design by Perseus Design

Paperback ISBN 978-1-908733-12-2
eBook ISBN 978-1-908733-13-9

Non Fiction / Metaphysics / Christian

Published by White Crow Books
www.whitecrowbooks.com

All bible texts are from the New Revised Standard Version,
Anglicized Edition (1995), unless otherwise indicated.

The front cover symbolizes the message of the book: green
and dark for the earth, white clouds for the interim period and
the sunlight behind the clouds the light of the new world.

# Contents

v

# Introduction

Is there life after death? This question is raised by many people, both believers and non-believers alike.

Surveys in the Netherlands have shown that 57% of church members (Roman-Catholic and Protestant) and 55% of the unchurched believe in a life after death.[1] It is remarkable that so few members and so many non-members believe this.

Even more remarkable is that in both categories more people believe in life after death than in God (40% among church members and 7% of non-members). Consider that church attenders, whenever they recite the Nicene Creed, affirm in the first line their belief in 'God, the Father, the Almighty' and in the last line their belief in 'the resurrection of the dead, and the life of the world to come'.

All this appears to indicate a considerable degree of 'wishful thinking' among the unchurched on the one hand and a rather confused belief among many church members on the other.

This seems to me sufficient reason to reconsider the question of life after death extensively and critically. The biblical grounds for the belief in life after death will be discussed. Other religions are also considered. In this context, I also discuss reincarnation belief that has come to us from eastern religions and that is accepted by 25% of church members in the Netherlands.[2]

Special attention is paid to the interim period between death and resurrection, a subject about which the Bible tells us little and on which most theologians remain silent. I consider therefore what we can learn from the so-called 'near-death experiences' about which there has been much discussion lately due to the work of scientists such as Pim van Lommel,[3] whose recent book, *Consciousness Beyond life: The Science of the Near-Death Experience*, has received much attention. It appears to provide information about the interim period between death and resurrection, a subject about which the Bible tells us little and on which most theologians remain silent.

It is also useful to consider our scientific knowledge of life and its inescapable limitation even though science cannot answer the question whether there exists life afer death. This further requires a discussion of the images that bible and science present of the human person.

In this way I arrive at a novel answer to the question: "Is there life after death?"

# Chapter 1

# Ancient and Eastern Religions

## 1.1 Egypt

Already from prehistoric times (100,000-20,000 years ago) there are indications of a belief in a life after death in the form of jewellery and tools in graves.[1]

In the ancient Egyptian religion, one of the oldest documented religions, life after death played a significant role. At death parts of the soul, *ka* (body double) and *ba* (personality) were believed to go to the underworld, of which *Osiris* was the god. Osiris was not only a merciful judge of the dead, but he was also considered to be the giver of all life by means of the fertility-bringing floods of the Nile. The reed lands in the Nile delta were seen as the heavenly paradise (*Aaru*). While the soul remained in Aaru, Osiris required labour from the dead as satisfaction for the protection rendered by him. Osiris was believed to have risen; the Pharaohs were thought be raised through him and later this was extended to all people who had performed the required labour.

Only souls that weighed less than the feather of the goddess *Maiat* were admitted to the long and dangerous journey to Aaru, where they then remained for ever in eternal bliss. Souls, who through their sins were heavier than the feather of Maiat, died a second death by being swallowed by the monster *Ammit*.

The Egyptians believed that mummification was required for receiving a life after death. Only a properly embalmed body, kept in a tomb made of blocks of clay (*mastaba*), made life possible in the fields of Aaru and accompanying the Sun on its daily journey. Later the pyramids for the pharaohs developed from the mastaba. In view of the deprivations ascribed to the afterlife in the *Book of the Dead*, food and jewellery were placed in the tomb.

## 1.2 Babylonia

The Babylonian religion is best known for its creation story *Enuma Elish*, elements of which are found in the description of the initial chaos in Gen.1:1-2. The Babylonian belief about the fate of the dead is much gloomier than that of the Egyptians. After death, the deceased person, wrapped in feathers like those of a bird sits lost in darkness. The land of the dead is surrounded by seven walls and ruled by queen *Erishkiggel*. Escape from it is impossible. But eventually the Babylonians expected to find the right ritual cure for death. This is expressed in the Ishtar myth, in which the goddess *Ishtar* after her death descends into the underworld. The earth then becomes lifeless and infertile. When Ishtar is raised by the magic song of *Eas,* she returns to the earth, which regains life and fertility. This myth presents a primitive belief in resurrection and life after death.

## 1.3 Zoroastrianism

In this ancient Persian religion, dating from the early second millennium BCE and based on the teaching of the prophet Zoroaster, *Ahura Mazda* is the all-good creator. He is not immanent, but is represented on earth by a multitude of messengers, called *Yazatas*. Good and evil have a different origin; evil attempts to destroy the good creation, while the good tries to maintain it.

In the teaching of Zoroaster it is assumed that the spirit (*urvan*) of a deceased person dwells for three days on earth before moving to the realm of the dead, ruled by *Yima*. The righteous spirit joyfully sings the *Ustavaiti Gathas*, whereupon a beautiful virgin appears, the personification of the good thoughts, words and deeds of the righteous spirit. Weeping the sinful spirit recites weeping the *Yasma*, whereupon an ugly, naked woman appears, the personification of the evil thoughts and deeds of the evil spirit. After three days the evil spirit is carried away by the demon *Vizaresa* over the *Chinvat* bridge to the darkness (hell).

*Yima* is the first king on earth and at the same time the first human who dies. In his empire of the dead the righteous spirits lead a shadowy existence, in which they are dependent on their descendants. The latter are to still the hunger of their dead parents and provide them with clothing by means of earthly rituals. Rituals during the first three days after death are to protect the spirit against evil powers. After three days the spirit reaches the Chinvat bridge, which is the site of the final judgment. *Rashnu* handles the scales of justice. If the good deeds of the deceased person outweigh his evil deeds, the spirit goes to paradise. In the reverse case the bridge narrows to a knife edge and an ugly witch carries the spirit to hell. If good and evil deeds balance each other, the spirit goes to a colourless existence without either joy or sorrow (*misvan gatu*).

## 1.4 Greeks and Romans

Ancient Greece knew many gods and stories about them, but lacked a uniform system of belief.[2] Thus Homerus describes in the *Odyssey* the dead as 'burnt-out phantoms' who if left without burial will keep roaming the earth as evil spirits, while Plato asserts in the myth of *Er* that the spirit of the deceased person is judged immediately after death and sent on, either to heaven as a reward or to the underworld as punishment.

Plato believes in an immortal spirit (soul) that is during life imprisoned in the body but escapes at death and then lives eternally After a period in heaven or hell the spirit is reincarnated.

Pythagoras, best known to us for his theorem of the right-angled triangle, also believed in reincarnation. After completion of the reincarnations the soul will sit at table with the gods.

Different ideas also existed about the underworld. Widely accepted was the idea of an underworld, named *Hades*, ruled by a god with the same name. It is a dark space between the place of torture and the place of rest. But there is also the idea of *tartarus*, the place of the doomed souls. Then there is the *Elysium*, a place of blissful life in eternal youth and eternal spring, but this restricted to the human descendents of the highest god *Zeus*.

Some heroes from Greek mythology were permitted to visit the underworld. In the myth of *Hercules* the hero must travel to the underworld to overpower the three-headed hellhound *Cerberus* and liberate *Alcetis*, the wife of *Admetus*.

The Roman religion was derived from a mixture of the Greek religion with Etruscan elements. Deities and cults were also acquired from conquered peoples. The Romans had similar ideas about life after death as the Greeks. The dream of *Scipio*, written by Cicero, describes what looks like an out-of-body experience: the spirit floats high above the earth and looks down on the small planet.

## 1.5 Germanic and Celtic religions

Polytheistic religions existed among the Germanic and North peoples from the iron-age until their conversion to Christendom. For the Germanics, *Wotan* was the highest god, while in the North it was *Odin*, who was also the god of death and magic.

The *Eddas*, written only in AD 1220, form the oldest source of information about life after death coming from the North. Various realms of the dead are described: 1. *Walhalla*, resembling the Elyseum of the Greeks, is the place for the warriors who died as heroes in wars; 2. *Hell*, similar to the Greek Hades, is the destination of those who distinguished themselves neither by good deeds, nor by evil ones, and who will be united with their loved ones; 3. *Niflhel*, similar to Tartarus of the Greeks, is thought to be below Hell and is the place for the punishment of those who had broken oaths, had raped women or had committed other evil deeds. Behaviour during life determined in which of these three places one would end up. Torture took place only in Nifthel. In the end everything would go up in flames in a final battle of the gods (Götterdämmerung), whereafter a new world would arise from the sea. A new, almighty race of gods would then rule over everything and everyone.

Not much is known about Celtic religious ideas because these were orally transmitted by the priests, the druids.[4] Originally the Celts were not aware of a heavenly judgment. They believed in realms of the dead and enchanted islands of the dead. The chief Celtic realm of the dead was a joyful spiritworld by the name of *Avalon*. There apples grew that would give eternal youth to those who ate them. Some Celts believed in reincarnation from Avalon. Dead warriors could be brought back to life in magic kettles.

## 1.6 Hinduism

The oldest Hindu writings, the *Vedas*, date from the period of 1700-1100 BCE and speak about the gods *Indra, Varuna* and *Agni*. Burnt offerings (*yajna*) were made and mantras were sung, but there were no temples and idols. The Vedic traditions show similarities with Zoroastrianism, which predates the Vedas.

Around 500 BCE the *Upanishads* appeared, which form the nucleus of present-day Hinduism. They provide the concepts of *Brahman* and *Atman*. Brahman is the universal mind, the source of all existence, from which the universe originates. Atman is the individual self, the mind of a living creature, particularly humans. In the *Advata* tradition Brahman and Atman are seen as one and the same. Change is considered an illusion since this cannot be reconciled with a permanent and homogeneous reality. Our purpose in life is to become aware of ourselves (atman) as identical with the uppermost mind (Brahman).

The Upanishads describe reincarnation (*punarjanma*) as an event after death. The sum of our good and evil deeds determines how we shall be reborn (*karma*). A good life is rewarded in the reincarnation, but after a bad life even reincarnation as an animal is possible. Krishna says in the *Bhagavad Gita* that like a person throws away old clothes and puts on new ones, so the soul casts off the old body and takes on a new body. The body is only a shell; the soul within the shell is unchangeable and indestructible and assumes different lives in the cycle of birth and death. After many cycles the soul becomes aware that worldly pleasures do not bring a deep and lasting joy (*ananda*) and begins to long for higher pleasures. When all desires have disappeared, the cycle ends and the soul reaches *moksha*, something like the state of redemption in christendom. The soul then 'dissolves' in *nirvana*, a state of perfect peace and transparency but without personal identity, so it is not a resurrection.

## 1.7 Buddhism

This religion was founded around 500 BCE in northeast India by Siddharta Gautama, who became known as the Buddha (he who is awakened). According to tradition he was born in 583 BCE in a prominent, wealthy family. At the age of 29 he left the parental home and began to wander around. During his wanderings he discovered the suffering of the sick and the elderly. His encounter with an ascetic saint led him to a meditative life. Ten years later, while meditating under a bodhi tree, he decided not to stand up until he received enlightenment (*nirvana*). After many days he succeeded in liberating himself from the cycle of reincarnation and rose up as a fully enlightened man. He attracted followers and founded a monastic order with them. During the rest of his life he traveled around to acquaint others with the path of enlightenment. He died at the age of 80 in Kushinagar, India.

When Buddhism reached China, it encountered the teachings of Confucius (551-478 BCE) with its moral, social, political and philosophical thoughts. Important elements of Confucianism were incorporated and thus Zen Buddhism originated, the form in which it arrived in Japan.

Buddhism, like Hinduism, has *karma*, the cycle of life, death and reincarnation. However, it believes that one can find liberation from this cycle in this life through meditation and detachment, and that it is possible to reach *nirvana* (or a state close to it).

The Tibetan Book of the Dead (*Bardo Thödol*),[3] dating from around 750 AD, teaches how to bring the soul of a deceased person safely to reincarnation. It describes what we shall experience during the dying process. It also contains chapters about the signs of death and the rituals to be performed when death is approaching or has already occurred. All of this is directed to liberation from this life and peaceful incorporation into the new life. It covers the period of 49 days (*bardo*) between death and reincarnation. One was supposed to study the book during one's life. During the dying process a *lama* (priest) read it into the ear of the dying person so as to be heard by the soul.

## 1.8 Islam

Of the three Abrahamitic faiths, Judaism, Christendom and Islam, I shall discuss the first two extensively in chapters 2 and 3. Here I confine myself to the Islamic belief in life after death. Islam ('subjection to God') was developed in the early seventh century from Judaism and early Christendom by the prophet Mohammed. He gave the name *Allah* to God and used parts of the Old and New Testament in writing the *Koran*, the holy book of Islam. In the Koran Abraham, Moses and Jesus are seen as prophets. The goal of humans is to worship Allah as the creator of heaven and earth, and to love their neighbours. Everything that happens in this world is only of importance in the light of the coming life.

There will be an end of time, an Apocalypse as is also known in the Bible. *Al-Dajjal* (Satan) may rule over the earth for forty years. Then the Messiah – that is Jesus of Nazareth according to the Koran – will return to earth. He defeats Dajjal and then the present world will pass away. Only Allah knows when this will take place.

This will be accompanied by a Day of Resurrection on which occasion judgment is passed. The Koran teaches a bodily resurrection at which all resurrected persons will have the age of 33 years, the age at which Jesus died and rose. There is a heaven (*jannah*) and a hell (*jahannam*), each with 7 levels. The highest level of heaven is paradise, a place of joy and bliss according to the Koran. Sins such as disbelief, dishonesty and usury can condemn a person to hell. The final destiny for everyone is an eternal realm that comprises both heaven and hell.

About the interim period between death and resurrection the Koran says only that the situation of the dead depends on their faith in Allah and on their deeds during life. According to Mohammed the soul rests during the interim period in the grave. Later a belief arose that the dead go immediately to heaven or hell; this would apply in particular for martyrs.

According to traditional interpretations of the Koran, only men would have access to paradise. Some Muslim theologians believe that women will be recreated as virgins who can please the men in paradise. Each martyr would have 72 virgins at his disposal. This may have inspired suicide terrorists to commit their evil deeds.

Islam also has a doctrine of predestination. Anything happening in this world whether good or bad, is predestined by Allah and nothing can happen without his approval. Muslim theologians claim nevertheless that humans have a free will in the sense that they can choose between good and evil and thus are responsible for their actions.

## 1.9 Conclusions and summary

All religions described in this chapter, whether ancient or current, have a belief in life after death, although the details vary widely. The least outspoken on this subject is the Babylonian religion, although the Ishtar myth suggests a resurrection and a continuing life.

All religions discussed, except Hinduism and Buddhism, place the continuing life in either a heaven or a hell, depending on behaviour during life in this world. In the two eastern religions further life takes place after reincarnation in a different being, higher after good behaviour and lower after bad behaviour in the preceding life. Ultimate destiny is to reach nirvana with loss of personal identity.

What is striking is that none of these religions, except to some extent Islam, speaks about the interim period between death and judgment. Equally striking is that none of these religions seems to know something resembling the Christian idea of redemption.

# Chapter 2

# Judaism

## 2.1 History of Israel

A number of small Semitic nomad tribes fled from Egypt around 1200 BCE and, after a long journey, settled in Canaan, the area between the Mediterranian Sea and the Jordan river. Around 1000 BCE these tribes chose a king named Saul, reasoning that under a king they could better defend themselves against the surrounding hostile communities. This king was Saul who was succeeded by David and then by his son Solomon. After the death of Solomon in 925 BCE the kingdom split in two parts, the North with Samaria as capital and the South, Judea, with Jerusalem as capital.

The weakened, divided Israel was subject for centuries to occupations and even deportations by its powerful surrounding countries. In 721 BCE Assyria occupied Samaria until it was itself defeated by Egypt in 660 BCE. In 597 BCE Babylonia occupied Judea and Samaria and appointed vassal kings. Because of collusions of these vassals with Egypt the Babylonians destroyed

Jerusalem in 587 BCE and deported almost the entire Jewish population to Babylon. In 539 BCE the Persians occupied Babylon. The Persian king Cyrus allowed the Jewish exiles to return to Judea and Samaria, which was now under Persian control. In 330 BCE Alexander the Great defeated the Persian empire, resulting in the hellenisation of the Near East. The successors of Alexander, first the Ptolemies of Egypt and, from 198 BCE, the Seleucids of Damascus and Antioch, ruled over Israel until 63 BCE. Then Pompey defeated the Seleucides and the Romans occupied Israel. All these events had their influences on the Hebrew culture and religion.

According to biblical tradition Moses had an encounter on Mount Sinai (Horeb) with the god Jahweh, who commanded him to lead the people Israel out of Egypt. During the so-called Exodus they settled for some time at the foot of Mount Sinai. After another encounter with Jahweh, Moses returned from the mountain with the Ten Commandments and other rules of life. He then had the people make a covenant (contract) with Jahweh, in which they recognized him as their god and the only god and promised to keep his commandments. Later, while Moses journeyed to the mountain top again, some of the people made a golden calf to worship. After his return, Moses had the apostates put to death. Infidelity to Jahweh occurred at times during the entire history of Israel. For instance, Solomon built shrines for Astarte, Milcom, Chemosh and Molech (1Kings 11:1-8). The prophets Jeremiah (2:19) and Zephaniah (1:4-6) also speak about infidelity to Jahweh.

## 2.2 The human image

Before discussing the Jewish ideas about death and life after death, it is necessary to consider the Jewish thinking about the human image. From the two creation stories in Genesis 1 and 2 we have become familiar with the thought that humans are entirely different and higher beings compared to animals. In the older story in Gen.2:4b-25 (circa 900 BCE) the human male, Adam, is created first and then the animals as his 'helpers'. But they do not fit Thereafter God creates the woman, Eve, from the flesh of Adam to become his companion. In the later story in Gen.1:1-33, 2:1-4a (circa 500 BCE) God first creates all plants and animals and finally the first human pair 'in his image'. God blesses the humans (but not the animals) and gives them dominion over all the earth and all living beings.

From here on I use the word 'mind' instead of 'soul' because the latter word can have two meanings: the life principle that is thought to leave us at death (Gen. 35:18) but also the self as the subject of desire and emotion (Mk.14:34; Lk.1:46).[1] Therefore I prefer to speak about the 'mind' of humans which I define as the complex of capabilities permitting us to observe, memorize, evaluate, make decisions, and to have emotions and religious experiences.

The word mind in this sense is translated from the Hebrew word *leb* (literally 'heart'), which is used a number of times in the Old Testament. It stands for the inner human, in the sense of courage, joy, sorrow, arrogance, compassion, excitement and desire, but also intelligence, will and religious stance. In the King James version *leb* is translated as 'heart' in a few places (2 Samuel 14:1; 1Kings 3:9), but in most places as 'mind'

(1Sam. 2:35; Isa.65:17; Jer.3:16, 19:5). In the NRSV 'mind' is also used in 2 Samuel 14:1 and 1Kings 3:9.

So the word *leb* is translated in modern English versions of the Bible as the indication of the human mind in all its various activities. In a few cases the Hebrew text uses the name of another organ: *kelaioth* (kidneys), *me'im* (intestines), and *kabed* (liver). Not mentioned is the word brain, since the brain was believed to be the 'marrow' of the skull; the true function of the brain was not yet understood in those days.

There is no Hebrew word for the living body. The nearest equivalent is *basar* (flesh). Basar is alternately translated as 'flesh' (Ps.119:120), 'body' (Eccl.2:3) or 'bones' (Prov.14:30). Flesh and bones are seen as the instruments used by our feelings. All this indicates that the Jews in the Old Testament time considered the mind as a component of the body without believing it to be localized in one particular organ. The living human being was seen as a unity of body and mind.

The idea of the body-mind unity was taken over in the New Testament (chapter 3.1), but it is also confirmed by our current neurobiological understanding of the role of specific neuronal networks in observing, processing, memorizing and communicating data. Some neurobiologists, however, go so far as to equate body and mind. An example is the Dutch neuroscientist Dick Swaab who published a book with the provocative title "We are our brain".[2] This is an unwarranted form of reductionism ("nothing but"). The mind cannot be equated with the neuronal networks in the brain, although it utilizes them for its operations in the living human being. The brain is the biological substrate for the mind. This distinction will appear again in our discussion of the so-called near-death experiences in chapter 6 and of the interim period between our death and resurrection in chapter 7.

Now the question arises: How does the human mind come to life? For this 'life-giving principle' three virtually synonomous words are used in the Old Testament: *nephesh, neshamah* and *ruach*. The first word, *nephesh*, is translated as 'life' (1Kings19:10), as the 'soul' that leaves the body at death (Gen.35:18) or as the 'breath of life' that returns to God at death (Eccl.12:7).

The word *neshamah* is translated as 'breath' in 1Kings17:17 and Job 27:3 and as God's 'breath of life' in Gen.2:7. The word *ruach*, which has the threefold meaning of wind, breath and spirit, is used as 'wind' in Ex.10:13, as 'spirit' in Judg.15:19 and 1Sam.30:12, and as Yahweh's 'breath' in Ex.15:8 (actually: 'the blast of your nostrils'), Isa.30:28 and Ezek.37:10. *Ruach* also stands for the inspiring of prophecy (1Sam.10:6) and of extraordinary power (Judg 14:6), and the loss of it leads to Saul's insanity (1Sam. 16:14). In Isa.26:9 we find *ruach* and *nephesh* in a single verse, translated as 'my soul' and 'my spirit', respectively.

From this survey of Old Testament texts we may conclude that the word *leb* represents the human mind in its various activities, while the words *nephesh, neshamah* and *ruach* mean 'life principle', God's breath of life that makes humans (and all other organisms) come to life and that is withdrawn at the moment of death.

## 2.3 Death and resurrection

In the Old Testament we can trace a clear development in the thinking about death.[3] In the earlier writings death is seen as the normal end of life (Job 5:26), if one is at a ripe old age and leaves children (Job 42:16-17). One is then 'united with one's ancestors' (Gen.25:8). The continuing life of the tribe was considered more important than that of the individual. Viewed in this perspective, what happened to an individual after death was not of great importance.

Once thinking about this arose, death came to be connected with the return of the life-giving spirit to God (*ruach*; Eccl. 12:7). There is, however, no text that justifies the assumption that at the moment of death the mind is separated from the body. The Jewish idea of the unity of body and mind, as described in the previous section, violates such an assumption. The cessation of respiration as well as of the ability to communicate with others were seen as an indication that both body and mind die when God withdraws his life-giving spirit.

During the next stage of thinking there came a growing awareness of the destructive aspect of death. An untimely death was seen as the work of an evil power and there were calls on Jahweh to save his followers from death (Ps.18:6-7; Ps.116:3-4). This hostile power was sometimes described as death coming in through the windows (Jer.9:20) or as the angel of death (2Sam. 24:16). But God retains the ultimate power over life and death. Punishment in the hereafter was not yet considered, because Jahweh was believed to punish individual sinners or the entire people Israel during life through illness, famine or foreign invasion.

Subsequently, the thought arose that the dead sojourned as shadows in a gloomy realm of the dead, *Sheol*, where God cannot be praised (Ps.6:5; Ps.115:17; Isa.38:18) and the voice of God cannot be heard (Ps.28:1; Ps.88:12). The prophet Amos proclaims that God's power also reaches into Sheol (Amos 9:2). Because death cannot exist in the presence of God, the thought arises that the dead 'sleep' (Jer.51:39, 57) and at some time they will awake (Job 19:25-27; Isa.26:19). In Dan. 12:2 this is connected with a judgment: *Many of those who sleep in the dust of the earth shall awake, some to everlasting life, and some to shame and everlasting contempt.* Here, a first hesitant and vague announcement of a resurrection, individually or as a people (Ezek. 37), appears in the Old Testament.[4] However, in the time of Jesus the Sadducees still denied the resurrection of the dead.

In the later development of Judaism the mind is seen as immortal.[5] At death the mind separates from the body to be reunited with it in the resurrection. The resurrection of the dead was professed in the last of the 13 articles of faith formulated by Moses Maimonides (1134-1204). For Hisdai Crescas (1340-1410) it was only a 'belief', because the highest ideal of Judaism is to serve God without any expectation of a reward. In modern Judaism the belief in the resurrection is maintained by orthodox Jews, but not by liberal Jews.

## 2.4 Conclusions and summary

After a brief sketch of the history of Israel, the Old Testament image of the human is discussed. Humans are considered to be higher beings than the animals, they are created in the image of God and given dominion over the earth and all its creatures. Humans are seen as consisting of body and mind. I avoid the word 'soul' because it can have two meanings: the self, but also the life-principle given by God. I define the mind as the complex of capabilities permitting us to observe, memorize, evaluate, make decisions, and to have emotions and religious experiences.

For 'mind' the Hebrew text uses the word *leb* (literally 'heart'), and occasionally another organ (kidneys, intestine, liver). The Hebrew language doesn't have a word for the living body; the word *basar* (flesh) is used to express that flesh and bone are the instruments that the mind makes use of. The Jews considered the living human as a body-mind unity. This idea is continued in the New Testament, particularly by Paul. The unity of body and mind is confirmed by our current neurobiological insight in the role of specific neuronal networks for observing, processing, memorizing and communicating data. These neuronal networks form the biological substrate for the activity of the mind. Neurobiologists, who consider brain and mind as identical are guilty of unwarranted reductionism.

The body-mind unity comes to life when God gives it the breath of life. Hebrew scripture has three nearly synonymic words for the breath of life: *nephesj, neshamah* and *ruach*. At death the breath of life is withdrawn.

A clear development, as to the nature of death and resurrection, is noticeable in the Old Testament. In the earlier writings death is seen as a natural end whereupon we are united with our ancestors. The survival of the tribe was considered more important than that of the individual. A further development is the thought that at death the breath of life returns to God with the death of both body and mind. Death was thought to be the work of a hostile power, the angel of death, against which the help of Jahweh was invoked.

Next the thought arose that the dead sojourn in a realm of the dead, named *Sheol*, where God cannot be praised, nor even be heard. As there can be no death in the nearness of God, it began to be thought that the dead 'sleep' and that at some time they will be raised. The prophet Daniel connects this with a judgment. This is the first, hesitant proclamation of a resurrection of the dead, individually or as a people. In the time of Jesus the Sadducees still denied the resurrection of the dead.

In later Judaism most rabbis see the mind as immortal and believe that at the resurrection it will be reunited with the body. This is currently the position of orthodox Judaism. Liberal Jews see this as merely a 'belief', whereas the highest ideal of Judaism is to serve God without any expectation of a reward.

# Chapter 3

# Christendom

## 3.1 The human image

The human image in the New Testament hardly differs from that in the Old Testament (ch.2.2). Here the human personality is also seen as a body-mind unity, particularly in the letters of Paul and the synoptic gospels (Mark, Matthew, Luke).[1,2]

Paul offers the most extensive treatment of the subject. He uses three words: *kardia, pneuma* and *nous*. For Paul, the word *kardia* (lit. heart) means personality, character, inner life (*the secrets of the unbeliever's heart*, 1Cor.14:25), the seat of the intellectual and spiritual activities (Rom.1:21) and will power (*your hard and impenitent heart*, Rom.2:5). For Paul *pneuma* and *nous* are the thinking, reasoning, reflecting, and purposeful aspect of the human self, the mind, while the body (*soma*) is the self and the object of these activities. The 'mind' permits us to understand God's revelation and to act in accordance with it. The human mind (*nous*) can be debased (Rom.1:28; 1Tim.6:5) but can also be renewed (Rom. 12:2). For Paul the mind encompasses the entire human being and can be considered the equivalent of 'character'. He uses the word *nous* (Rom. 11:34; 1Cor.2:16) for the thinking and the intellectual ability of humans, and it can be morally good as well as bad. In 1Cor.14:14f *nous* is translated as 'mind' and *pneuma* as 'spirit'; in Phil.4:7 *nous* is tanslated as 'understanding' and *kardia* as 'heart'.

For the Hebrew word *nephesh* Paul uses the word *psyche* and for *ruach* the word *pneuma*. *Psyche* is translated simply as 'life' (Phil. 2:30), as life that brings 'anguish and distress' (Rom.2:9), in the sense of 'from the heart' (Ef.6:6) and as 'soul' (1Thess. 5:23). In these three texts *psyche* means the emotional side of consciousness. *Pneuma* is commonly used by Paul to mean 'supernatural influences', and occasionally for the 'life principle'. He often uses the word to mean 'human spirit', however in Rom.8:16 he uses the word *pneuma* for God's Spirit as well as for the human spirit (*that very Spirit bearing witness with our spirit*).

In the synoptic gospels there is – compared to Paul – a change in emphasis but not in content. Jesus emphasizes the need for a spiritual life (Lk.10:38-42) and not so much for an ascetic life (Mt.11:19). Justice, mercy and faith are to him the most important aspects of the Law (Mt.23:23). For John, on the other hand, Christ brings the light of life into a world full of darkness (Jn.8:12, Jn. 12:46). He distinguishes between sinfulness as a character trait (*a slave to sin*, Jn.8:34) and the committing of a specific sin that can be forgiven (1Jn.1:9). The latter requires our moral will to 'purify ourselves' (1Jn.3:3).

The later theological discussion about the human mind has been mainly directed to the 'soul' and its role in sin and redemption. The thinking at the time was strongly influenced by Greek philosophy, successively Stoicist, Platonist and Aristotelian. The following summatries demonstrate that the 'soul' was considered virtually the same as the human mind, as defined in ch.1.1.

Tertullian (circa 200), influenced by stoicism, sees the soul as an entity with many functional activities of which intellect and will are the highest. The soul is for him localized in the heart, while the body is merely the instrument of the soul.

Clement of Alexandria (circa 200), under platonic influence, believes in a tripartite soul, consisting of one part intellect (*nous*, divine and immortal), one part passion, and one part desire.

Origen (circa 225), also a Platonist, assumes a unity of body, soul and mind, which brings him close to the thinking of Paul.

Gregory of Nyssa (circa 370) proceeds from the Aristotelian form of a soul with vegetative, animal and intellectual parts, independent of the body.

Augustine (354-430) adopts Origen's idea of a unity of body, soul and mind. He believes the soul is created by God but is transferred from parent to child. This transfer is a confirmation of the doctrine of original sin proposed by Origen.

Thomas Aquinas (1225-74) also believes that the soul is created and inserted in the body by God. He does not believe in a transfer of the soul from parent to child. The soul is capable of acquiring merits but only with the action of divine grace. Thomas accepts free will, but states that it cannot be addressed to God unless God converts it to himself.

Duns Scotus (1264-1308) emphasizes the will, divine as well as human, rather than the intellect as Thomas does. The will serves to maintain order in the rebellious nature of humans that is corrupted through the Fall. He sees humans as a unity of body and soul in a unique individual. The soul is capable of intuitive knowledge of the spiritual life.

The Reformers have added little to our understanding of the human mind. Martin Luther (1483-1546) proclaims *sola fide*, justification through belief alone. Belief is for him a full trust in God rather than an intellectual assent. He believes in original sin and predestination.

Philip Melanchthon (1497-1560), the most prominent theologian of the Lutheran movement, brings a nuance to *sola fide* by recognizing the need for cooperation between God's Spirit and the human will in our conversion.

John Calvin (1509-64) maintains the loss of free will through the Fall. His strong emphasis on God's omnipotence and omniscience leads him to the doctrine of 'double predestination', i.e. before their creation God predestined some of his human creatures to redemption and others to eternal perdition. For me this doctrine is the lowest point in theological thinking about the human mind.

### 3.2 Death and resurrection

In the New Testament, particularly in Paul's writings, our mortality is seen as related to human sinfulness (*the sting of death is sin*, 1Cor.15:56; *the wages of sin is death*, Rom.6:23). Paul bases this idea – incorrectly — on Gen.2 and 3. Although in Gen.2:9 in addition to the tree of the knowledge of good and evil the tree of life is mentioned, only the eating of the fruit of the first-mentioned tree is forbidden (Gen.3:3). Loss of immortality is not mentioned among the punishments allotted by God to Adam and Eve for eating the forbidden fruit (Gen.3:16-19). Only later, when God chases Adam and Eve from Paradise, it is said that this is to *prevent* them from eating the fruit of the tree of life and thus becoming immortal (Gen.3:22-24). The humans created by God were not immortal at any point. Gen.2:17 should not — according to most exegetes — be read as an indication that humans were initially immortal. At best one might conclude from Gen.3 that Adam and Eve through their disobedience lost the *possibility* of becoming immortal. Furthermore, we should consider that Gen.2 and 3 are mythical stories and thus we should be cautious about drawing literal conclusions from them.

The resurrection of Christ is seen in the New Testament as a unique event, as the resurrection of the Messiah.[4] Paul ascribes the resurrection of the human dead to that of Christ (1Cor.15:22). But he also says that if there were no resurrection of the dead, then Christ would not have risen either (1Cor.15:13). I do not find the latter two claims strong, since Christ is the divine Son of God. Peter is a little more cautious: *By his great mercy he* [God] *has given us a new birth into a living hope through the resurrection of Jesus Christ from the dead* (1Pet.1:3). Through his death and resurrection Christ opened the heavenly kingdom to all believers (Eph. 2:5-6; Heb.10:20). In Jn.10:10 Jesus says: *I came that they may have life, and have it abundantly.* Paul connects our justification to the resurrection of Christ (Rom. 4:25).

However, our resurrection awaits the return of Christ (*parousia*) at the coming of the new world (1Cor.15:23). For Paul this expectation was so central that he says to the governor Felix: *It is about the resurrection of the dead that I am on trial before you today* (Acts 24:21). Paul also says that we are now already transformed towards the resurrection life through the action of the Spirit (2Cor.3:18). About the resurrection body Paul poses that it will be radically different from our transitory earthly body and that God will choose the form for each one of us (1Cor.15:37-49). In 2Cor.5:3 Paul seems to allude to the interim period between death and resurrection when he says: *when we have taken it* [the earthly body] *off we will not be found naked*. Very little is said in the Bible about the interim period, probably because Jesus and his disciples expected the last day to occur in their time. Meanwhile we, living 2000 years later, are still expecting the return of Christ.

In ch.7 I shall extensively discuss the interim period.

Paul's argument that the resurrection of believers follows from the resurrection of Christ (1Cor.15:22) is not compelling in my opinion. After all, we believe that Christ is the Son of God and then his resurrection is to be expected: the divine cannot remain in the fetters of death. But the resurrection of the human dead – who are not divine – does not necessarily follow from the resurrection of Christ. In my opinion our resurrection derives from the doctrine of creation, which tells us that the world and all living creatures, including humans, were created out of love by God. The mortality of all living beings was necessary to enable the evolution of life from protocell to humans. But God will not leave it at that. The doctrine of creation also tells us that God is bringing his creation to perfection, to the new world. This will include the raising of the dead and their entrance into the new world, where there is no more mortality but eternity life. The risen Christ plays the role of the pioneer. Key to the new world is our belief in Christ.

The question of what will happen to those who have not come to know Christ during their lifetime will be discussed in chapter 7, which deals with the interim period between death and resurrection.

## 3.3 Later developments

Whereas the Bible says little about the period between our death and the resurrection of the dead on the last day, there arose in the twelfth century the idea of purgatory. Here the dead are subjected to horrible tortures in order to purge them from the sins committed during earthly life.[3] This is described in lurid detail in the journeys to the hereafter of St. Bandan and Tondalus,[4] and particularly of Dante Alighieri.[5] These stories were probably conceived in order to frighten simple believers into improving the quality of their lives.

The Reformation eliminated 'the bookkeeping of the masses for the dead and letters of indulgence' but, because of the predestination doctrine, people were anxious to know whether they belonged to the elect or the damned.

The Enlightenment brought a new development, whereby the Church lost more and more influence and the 'secularization of death' arose. The hereafter became less frightening, hell retreated to the background and the eschatological meeting with loved ones became more important than meeting God.

In the twentieth century death is being 'professionalized' in the sense that physician and undertaker take over the helm from the pastor. Palliative care and euthanasia, at home or in a hospice, and mourning care make their entrance. Where the 'in memoriam' card, common in Roman-Catholic circles, was traditionally composed by the priest and included a request to pray for the repose of the soul of the deceased person, it is now usually a farewell message written by the next-of-kin or the undertaker. The funeral service is now more directed at the relatives than at the deceased person and is now often conducted without a pastor at the funeral center rather than in church. A healthier tendency, particularly in Anglican circles, is to make the funeral service a celebration of the life of the deceased person.

### 3.4 Revolt against death

Those who do not believe in the biblical message about death and the future life, or are not even aware of it, are inclined to feel a resistance against death. They see death as an evil that should not exist. Our mortality is, however, a natural phenomenon that is necessarily connected with the evolution of life. Without the mortality of all living beings, natural selection could not operate and the evolution of life from protocell to humans could not have taken place. Death is therefore not an evil in a theological sense.

Nevertheless, the death of a young child or of a parent of young children through illness or accident, remains a tragic loss. In such cases one could call this an evil. The death of an elderly person, even though this may be the immediate result of illness, is the inescapable consequence of our mortality. It is an event for which we should prepare ourselves during our lifetime and about which we may know on biblical grounds that it will lead to a new life that knows no more death. Thus it has been ordained by God, who created us through evolution in order to grant us eternity life[6] at the completion of his creative work.

The humanist philosopher Christa Anbeek, after the sudden loss of her partner, has searched for the meaning of death, apart from its biological necessity.[7] In Zen Buddhism that teaches us to live without support, she found no consolation for her loss. She then sought counsel from the existential psychotherapy of the American psychiatrist Irvin Yalom, the classical art of life of Joep Dohmen and Wilhelm Schmid, the writings of philosopher Patricia de Martelaere, the authors Kristien Hemmerechts and Anna Enquist, cardiologist Pim van Lommel on near-death experiences, the poets Rutger Kopland and Thich Nhat Hanh, and the atheist evolutionary biologist Richard Dawkins. She presents their thoughts about life and death tersely, but she also looks critically at their philosophies and compares them to her own experience. Her conclusion in the end is: "I have no answer to death. There is no sense in death. From it all it appears that there is only sense in life". To which I would like to add: and in the future life. Unfortunately, this lies outside her scope.

### 3.5 Conclusions and summary

In the New Testament humans are seen as a unity of body and mind as in the Old Testament. This is particularly true for the letters of Paul and for the synoptic gospels of Mark, Matthew and Luke. For the Hebrew word *leb*

Paul uses the word *kardia* (heart), meaning personality, inner life, and seat of intellectual and spiritual activities, in other words the human mind. For *nephesh, neshamah* and *ruach* (breath of life) he uses the words *psyche, pneuma* and *nous*, understood as life, the emotional side of consciousness, and the life principle.

Later theological discussions about the human mind were virtually entirely directed to the 'soul' and its role in sin and redemption. The thinking was strongly influenced by Greek philosophy. Tertullian sees the soul as an entity with several functional activities, particularly intellect and will, localized in the heart. The body is only an instrument of the soul. Clement of Alexandria believes in a tripartite soul with one part for the intellect, one for passion, and one for desire. Origen assumes a unity of body, soul and mind, coming close to Paul. Gregory of Nyssa proceeds from a soul with vegetative, animal and intellectual parts, independent of the body. Augustine follows Origen in assuming a unity of body, soul and mind. He believes the soul to be created by God, but transferred from parent to child, through which he confirms Origen's doctrine of original sin. Thomas Aquinas rejects the transfer of the soul from parent to child. He accepts free will, but claims that it cannot be addressed to God unless God converts it to himself. Duns Scotus sees humans as a unity of body and soul in a unique individual, the soul being capable of intuitive knowledge of the spiritual life. The human will serves, according to Aquinas, to keep order in the rebellious human nature that is debased through the Fall. The Reformers have added little to our understanding of the human mind.

Ascribing our mortality to the Fall, as Paul does, is not correct. Nowhere in Gen. 2 and 3 is it said that humans have ever been immortal. His ascribing human resurrection on the last day to the resurrection of Christ is logically not strong: the rising of Christ, the divine Son of God, is a unique event that need not necessarily lead to our resurrection. It can, however, be said that through our belief in Christ we shall participate in his resurrection. In 1Cor.15 Paul says that our resurrection awaits the return of Christ (*parousia*) that will lead to the transformation of this world into the new kingdom. He also speaks there about the resurrection body that we shall receive.

About the interim period between our death and resurrection the Bible remains virtually silent, presumably because Jesus and his disciples expected the return during their time. Since the interim period has now already lasted 2000 years, it is important to pay attention to it (ch.7). In the Middle Ages this led to the idea of purgatory. The Reformers emphasized predestination. All this led to anxious thoughts about death and the hereafter. The Enlightenment led to changes but also to secularisation. In the 20th century death became 'professionalized': physician and undertaker replace the priest, the funeral center replaces the church.

Secularisation also leads to a revolt against death as an evil that should not exist. The mortality of all living beings is, however, required for the evolution from protocell to human. Death is, therefore, not an evil in the theological sense. It is an event for which we should prepare ourselves during our lifetime and about which we know from the biblical message that it will lead to a new life without death. Thus it has been ordained by God who created us through the evolutionary process and who will give us eternity life upon the completion of his creative work.

# Chapter 4

# Reincarnation and Parapsychology

### 4.1 Reincarnation

Reincarnation is the belief that after death the human mind or soul passes into another body, either human or animal. This leads to a new personality but a part of the old 'self' is retained in the successive lives.

This is a key doctrine of eastern religions, particularly Hinduism and Buddhism (see ch. 1, sections 6 and 7). In recent decades reincarnation belief has found some acceptance in the West, first among New Age adherents and now among many adherents of the 'new spirituality'. Since in the Netherlands and the USA nearly one quarter of church members claim to believe in reincarnation, a critical study of this religious phenomenon is warranted. First I describe the forms in which reincarnation belief has appeared in different religions and religious currents.

## Hinduism

Hindus believe that the soul (*atman*) is immortal, while at death the body is cast off as a worn garment. *Atman* then takes on a new body according to *karma*, the force that determines the cycle of death and rebirth (*samsara*). After many cycles *atman* begins to understand that worldly pleasures cannot bring deep and lasting joy (*ananda*) and begins to long for higher joys. When all desires have disappeared, the cycle ends and the soul achieves *moksha*, something resembling the state of redemption in the Christian religion. *Atman* then dissolves in *nirvana*, a state of perfect peace and transparency, but without personal identity. There is no resurrection.

## Buddhism

There is a clear difference between the Buddhist and Hindu versions of the reincarnation doctrine. In the Buddhist version there is no surviving *atman* that takes on a new life. At the death of an individual a new person comes into being, like when a new candle is lit with a candle that is burning out (*anatta*). So there is no transmigration in the strict sense. What is reborn is an evolving consciousness. A newborn child can be the reincarnation of a deceased prominent *lama*. One can also be reborn as an animal, depending on behaviour in the preceding life and spiritual condition at death. At long last there comes an end to the cycles when the soul has reached a spiritual state in which it is free of desires and anger, is at peace with the world and has compassion for everyone else. Then it passes into *nirvana*, as in the Hindu version.

## New Age and new spirituality

New Age is a Western spiritual movement that arose in the second half of the twentieth century.[1] It draws upon both Eastern and Western spiritual and metaphysical traditions, infused with influences from self-help, motivational psychology, holistic health, parapsychology, consciousness research and even quantum physics. Reincarnation was taken over from Eastern religions but in an adapted form. *Karma* as inescapable fate becomes an opportunity for further spiritual growth on a path that offers new opportunities. It is a progressive belief through which we bring about our own redemption and in which our reincarnations mark the stages of our spiritual growth. This fits with the New Age view of Jesus as a prophet who points the way to wholeness, rather than as the Redeemer who brings about reconciliation between God and humans.

This Western version of reincarnation also fits into the so-called 'new spirituality', in which the search for God is replaced by the search for the 'better self'. In the Netherlands 25% of church members believe in reincarnation.[2] In the United States the percentage is only slightly lower (22%).[3] Of the adherents of the new spirituality in the Netherlands 49% believe in reincarnation.[4] There is even a new type of psychotherapist who bring their clients under hypnosis to search for an earlier existence. Some of these therapists do not believe in reincarnation themselves but claim that their clients lose psychical problems and get a better self-feeling, faster and cheaper than through psychoanalysis.

### Is reincarnation belief compatible with the Christian faith?

Some New Age authors claim that the early Church mistakenly rejected reincarnation on the basis of a misinterpretation of certain Bible texts and a decision of the

Council of Constantinople. There is, however, no biblical evidence for reincarnation. The New Age authors cite Ex. 20:5, where it is actually said that the children will be punished to the third and the fourth generation for the sins of the parents. This idea is, however, forcefully rejected by the prophet Ezekiel (Ezek.18:19-20) as well as by Jesus in Jn. 9:2 in the case of the blind man. The pious Jewish belief that the prophet Elijah will return (Mal. 4:5; Sir. 48:10) is not a case of reincarnation, but the belief that he will return as a forerunner of the coming Day of the Lord. This is also expressed in the New Testament in the belief of many that Elijah returned as John the Baptist (Mt. 11:14, 17:10-13) or as Jesus (Mt. 16:14; Lc. 9:8). There is not any basis for the claim of New Age authors that Emperor Constantine and his mother Helena had references to reincarnation removed from the New Testament. Origen developed an idea about the pre-existence of souls that seems to show some likeness to reincarnation, but this was rejected by Augustine (ca. 400), implicitly by the Council of Constantinople (553) and explicitly by the Councils of Lyons (1274) and Florence (1439). We may thus conclude that reincarnation has no biblical foundation and has been repeatedly rejected by the Church.

The biblical message is that we are created as unique persons, destined for resurrection on the last day to eternity life in communion with God in his new world. We are created as a unity of body and mind that shall return in a perfected state after our bodily resurrection. This stands in sharp contrast to the idea of a disembodied soul that after transplantation in different bodies will dissolve and disappear as an individual in a *nirvana*. Christians believe that our reconciliation with God rests entirely on his merciful gift of redemption in Jesus Christ and our acceptance of this gift in faith. *Karma*, either as fate (eastern version) or as assignment (New Age version), offers no solution: the fundamental point is that we cannot redeem ourselves. This is not only a biblical message but the personal experience of anyone who dares to face honestly his own imperfection over against a perfect God. Eastern religion, New Age thinking and new spirituality do not seem to know true forgiveness and divine mercy in this sense.

## Some critical questions about reincarnation

About the 'process' of reincarnation some critical questions can be asked that its adherents seem to overlook.

(1) What happens to the soul of the being into which my soul is to be reincarnated: change places or 'two natures'?

(2) If I would be an incarnation of Napoleon, then I should have his genome, but where then does my genome remain?

(3) Does my reincarnated soul remember the sins for which I would be degraded to existing for instance as a spider? If not, how can I learn from the experiences of my past human life?

(4) How can my spider-goodness be transferred to the higher form?

(5) If we remember our previous existence (and that is needed in order to be able to do something with it in our new existence), why do so few people claim to have such a recollection?

In my opinion, the current popularity of the reincarnation idea stems from the quest for meaning and hope of those who have lost the Christian belief in resurrection to eternity life.

## 4.2 Parapsychology

This discipline studies paranormal phenomena that fall outside the regular, such as clairvoyance, telepathy and extrasensory perception. The practisers claim that they carry out their studies in scientific fashion. There are professional societies: 1882 the British Society for Psychical Research (SPR) since 1882, the American Society for Psychical Research (ASPR) since 1885, and the worldwide Parapsychological Association since 1957. There are also some professional journals, and some universities have chairs and research institutes in this field.

Some parapsychologists concern themselves with life after death. For instance, psychiatrist Ian Stevenson, University of Virginia, carried out extensive studies of reincarnation for almost 40 years until his death in 2007. His research was mainly focused on Asian children of 2 to 7 years. At the same university the possible existence of consciousness after physical death is currently being studied.

About communication with the dead much research has been done, in which many cases of fraud have been uncovered and others have produced rather trivial results. This is one reason for me to maintain a sceptical attitude to this phenomenon and not use it in my further study of life after death, in contrast to Michael Tymn.[5]

However, I shall describe one instance that has impressed me. It concerns a book published by the Anglican priest Michael Cocks about his conversations with Stephen, the first Christian martyr (Acts 7).[6] As a (non-professional) medium, Thomas Ashman received in the 1970s 174 messages from Stephen that were mainly tape-recorded by his wife Olive in a private circle in Christchurch, New Zealand, where Cocks was one of the questioners. Stephen mostly spoke in a strange kind of English, but sometimes in a Greek dialect spoken in Thrace. Cocks deduced from Stephen's use of a native Thracian word, and Greek word endings characteristic of that area, that his parents came from Thrace. However, Stephen said of himself that he was born near Ancyra in Galatia. Cocks concludes that the message of Stephen is profound but not novel: "It is our call to become the manifested love of God, an extension of the Father." To the question about God Stephen replied: "God is everything that you see and more, everything that you cannot imagine and picture. I feel that I am a part of this." The cautious reporting of Cocks and his thorough study of the descent of Stephen on the basis of the Greek words used by him lead me to believe the truth of this story. But what have we learnt from it? Really not much more than that there appears to be life after death and that in special cases a dead person can contact a living person. About the interim period in which Stephen would now exist, nothing is said by him.

Although the phenomenon of 'near-death experiences' can be considered to be a subject of parapsychology, I treat this subject separately and in more detail in ch. 6 in view of its role in my further argument.

## 4.3 Route map for the hereafter

A humorous summary of the main ideas about life after death has been composed in the form of the Paris metro map by Guido Derksen and Martin van Mousch with the assistance of cartographer Jop Mijwaard.[7] From the station Gare du Mort (station of death) four metro lines run to different corners of the city. The purple line stands for traditional Christendom. At Schism Street it splits in a line for Catholics and one for Protestants but these join again at the terminal station Heaven. When you travel on the purple line in the opposite direction you pass Porte d'Enfer (hell) and at Vale of Tears the line splits, one branch going to the terminal Forgiveness and the other to terminal Hell. A yellow line for modern theologians runs via Gare du Mort to the terminals Heavenly Emptiness and Nothingness. For the esoterics there is the blue line that runs in one direction via stations such as Celestine Promise, Sufism, Near-Death and Tunnel to Light. In the other direction it leads via stations such as Scientology, Anthroposophy, Wicca Bridge, Séance and Medium to Ghost Court. For the secularists there is a red line running from Gare du Mort via stations such as Dedication, Virtues Market, Philanthropy, Meeting Again, Blessed Ones to the terminal In the Clouds; in the opposite direction via Egoism, Jealousy, Intolerance, Violence Park, Sorrow, Loneliness and Torment to the terminal Doom Village. The river Seine, here called River of Life, forms the boundary between this world and the realm of the dead.

On other maps the ideas about the hereafter of Aztecs, Persians, Egyptians, Greeks, Hebrews, Germanics and Arabs are presented. The authors show that what was thought about the hereafter is often derived from the society in which one lives. For instance, the Norsemen and Germanics enjoy their warlike passions in Walhalla and indulge in wild boar and alcoholic beverages. Even though all the dead descend to an underworld, there are different positions. Some are rewarded, others are punished, depending on their behaviour during life. The realm of the dead is split into heaven and hell, for Christians as well as Muslims. We should liberate our thinking about life after death from all these too human fringes, the authors say in conclusion. This I shall attempt to do in the next chapters of this book.

## 4.4 Conclusions and summary

Reincarnation, the belief in a transmigration of the soul at death, enjoys great interest in western countries, nowadays. This is particularly true for adherents of the New Age movement and the new spirituality (49%), but even 25% of church members in the Netherlands and 22% in the United States say they believe in reincarnation.

Reincarnation belief stems from Hinduism and Buddhism. Hindus believe in an immortal soul (*atman*) that after death moves into a new body. After many cycles of death and rebirth the *atman* begins to realize that worldly pleasures cannot bring deep satisfaction. Then the cycle ends and the soul 'dissolves' in *nirvana*, a condition of perfect peace and transparency, but without the loss of personal identity. Buddhists believe that at death a new person originates, just as a new candle is lit with a candle that is burning out. Our behaviour in the preceding life determines what level of life we shall receive, possibly even becoming an animal.

New Age and the new spirituality have adopted the eastern reincarnation belief in a changed form. *Karma* as inescapable fate changes into an opportunity for further spiritual growth. The same is true for the new spirituality, where the search for God is replaced by the search for the 'better self'. These are forms of 'self redemption'.

There is no biblical evidence for reincarnation. New Age authors cite Ex. 20:5, where it is said that the sins of the parents will be visited upon the children, a thought that is forcefully rejected by Jesus (Jn.9:2). The pious Jewish belief that the prophet Elijah will return is not a case of reincarnation but a return as the forerunner of the coming Day of the Lord. In the New Testament many believe that Elijah returned as John the Baptist or as Jesus. Origen developed a thought about the precedence of souls, which shows some likeness to reincarnation but which was rejected by Augustine and three later Church councils.

The biblical message is that we are created as unique individuals, destined for resurrection on the last day to eternity life in full communion with God in his new kingdom. We are created as a unity of body and mind that will return in a perfected state after our resurrection. Reconciliation with God rests entirely on his merciful gift of redemption in Jesus Christ and our acceptance of this gift in faith.

Critical questions can be directed to the reincarnationists, e.g. if for bad behaviour I am reincarnated as a spider, how can this spider be aware of this and 'do better'?; what happens to my genome and that of the being in which I am reincarnated?

Communication with the dead through a medium remains a disputed matter. A report of conversations with the first Christian martyr Stephen obtains a certain degree of trustworthiness through the analysis of the Greek words. However, the conversations do not offer new insights, e.g. about the interim period in which Stephen now resides.

All ideas about the afterlife have been summarized in humorous fashion in the shape of a colourful Parisian metro map by Guido Derksen c.s.

# Chapter 5

# Biomedical Aspects
of Death

### 5.1 Biology of death

Our current biological knowledge can help us understand why humans are mortal, what leads to their inescapable death and even about the decomposition of the body after death. Biology cannot, however, answer the question whether there is life after death or not.

Death can occur rapidly in an accident or after a heart infarct. In diseases such as cancer the death process can take a long time. Death occurs when the most crucial vital functions, such as respiration, blood circulation and brain function, cease. The blood circulation is maintained by the pump function of the heart. The brain regulates the respiration; when the brain doesn't send stimuli, respiration slows down and eventually ceases entirely.

In cancer there are other factors that play a role. A tumour demands large amounts of nutrients that are withdrawn from the rest of the body. In addition treatments such as chemotherapy and radiation may lead to a decreased appetite. The patient loses weight and becomes cachectic, as the body attempts to obtain energy through the breakdown of muscle tissue. Decreased uptake of fluid and food lead to lower blood pressure, leading to a decreased blood supply to vital organs, which also leads to death. The resistance against infections decreases, often leading to pneumonia. In this case it can be ethically acceptable to withhold antibiotics and thus shorten the dying process.

When respiration ceases, life ends. When the heart has stopped pumping, body cells receive no oxygen anymore and die after some time, varying from a few minutes to a few days.

Then begins a process of decomposition that can be characterized in various stages.[1] Through lack of oxygen carbon dioxide accumulates in the cell, leading to acidification of the cell content. This leads to rupture of cell membranes, particularly those of the intracellular lysosomes. Enzymes located in the lysosomes are released and break down proteins and other biomolecules in the cell. Lack of oxygen makes muscle cells switch to glucose as energy producer, which produces lactic acid. After a few hours this produces muscle contraction and stiffness (*rigor mortis*).

The early decomposition phenomena make it necessary to remove organs for transplantation no later than one hour after death has been ascertained.[2] A number of rules have been established to prevent premature removal of organs: 1. Transplantation surgeons may enter the room only after other physicians have determined the death of the patient, 2. Organ removal may begin no sooner than 120 seconds after death has been declared, 3. Death is determined as cessation of respiration and heartbeat, 4.

In the case of artificial respiration a flat electroencephalogram, indicating brain death, is used as the criterion (85% of cases). Observance of these rules assures that no organs are removed from a living person.

## 5.2 Extension of life

In the last two centuries life expectancy at birth has increased dramatically, particularly in western countries. Worldwide it rose from 30 years in 1900 to 69 years in 2010, in the United States from 50 years to 79 years. In the Netherlands it rose from 37 years (!) in 1860 to 78 years in 2010. The much less favourable picture in developing nations I leave out of consideration, only noting that fortunately in those countries life expectancy is also increasing.

The increase of life expectancy is due in the first place to improved hygiene, in the second place to better nutrition and only in the third place to better medical care, particularly with the availability of antibiotics. In western nations the challenge for the medical profession is to provide a better life during the final years of life, rather than achieving a longer life. This will require better preventive care and a better treatment of patients with several chronic diseases (multimorbidity).[3]

The increasing life expectancy has several social consequences. One problem is to limit the ever-increasing costs of medical care for governments and citizens. The other problem is to safeguard the payment of public and private pensions to longer-living retired persons. For this reason the retirement age is being raised in many countries, e.g. from 65 to 67. However, this presupposes that employees are enabled to work that much longer.

It should also be kept in mind that I have spoken thus far about life expectancy at birth. The life expectancy of 65-year old males has only risen from 13.9 years in 1960 to 15.4 years in 2006.

Meanwhile many scientists are studying the possibility of further increasing our lifespan. Although humans live longer (122 years maximum) than most animals, some animals surpass us: the Galapagos marine tortoise can live 150 years, a whale species 210 years. Higher animals, such as the chimpanzee (59 years) have a shorter life span than humans. Little is known as yet about the causes for these differences in longevity.

What limits our life span? During life our cells are damaged in several ways.[4] DNA mutations occur, proteins such as enzymes are structurally damaged, free radicals (small, highly reactive molecules) rupture membranes, and so on. This leads to various diseases, especially in later life. In the brain memory decreases and reaction time increases. In the eyes cataract and nearsightedness occur. The heartbeat during exertion decreases. Vertebrae become damaged through many years of pressure. Bones show a net loss of bone mineral and thus break more readily. Joints lose cartilage, making the bones rub against each other resulting in painful arthrosis, sometimes aggravated by rheumatism. The leg arteries expand, causing accumulation of blood. Decreasing activity of insulin in the cells leads to diabetes 2 with the risk of many related complications. Many elderly people suffer from two or more chronic illnesses (multimorbidity): from 39% at age 55 to 95% above age 85.[3] It is clear that we have not been designed for an unlimited life span.

In addition, the number of cell divisions is limited to a maximum through the so-called telomeres. These are caps of 50 to 60 DNA molecules on top of each chromosome. At every cell division the telomere loses one DNA molecule. The cell has an enzyme, telomerase, that builds up the telomeres. However, in normal adults telomerase is inactive in the body cells. Could we perhaps increase our life span by activating telomerase? However, that might induce cancer. Telomerase activation is known to occur in tumour cells, allowing them to have unlimited cell division.

Then there is apoptosis, programmed cell death. This is a process that during embryonic development removes superfluous cells. In later life it leads a slumbering existence, only becoming active when a damaged cell must be removed. Cancer cells are able to inactivate the apoptosis process and thus to keep themselves alive. Theoretically it would be possible to activate apoptosis in the cells of an elderly person and thereby remove damaged cells, including cancer cells, before they could lead to disease processes. This would also be a risky undertaking, the profit of which would not be assured.

In worms, flies and mice it has been found that severe restriction of food intake after reaching adulthood considerably lengthens the life span. It is, however, unlikely that this would also work in humans, because we have a much slower and less easily regulated metabolism than these animals. Indirectly, a low-calorie diet has a life-extending effect by preventing cardiac illness and diabetes and their consequences.

In his book *The Physics of Immortality* physicist Frank J. Tipler proposes a mechanism for immortality and resurrection that he claims is in agreement with the physical laws.[5] He assumes that we will design extremely fast and powerful computers with a memory large enough to store digitally every intelligent being that has ever lived. These computers can then be sent to other galaxies in order to escape the heat death caused by our sun turning into a red giant after exhausting all its fuel (in about 5 billion years). From such a computer the life stored in its memory can be brought to a virtual reality, to 'resurrection'. In order to make his story acceptable to Jewish and Christian believers, he poses an omega point, i.e. the Jewish-Christian God who governs all this. This for him is not a belief but physics, just as he considers theology a subdivision of physics. Tipler expects that the colonization of the entire universe by these computers will allow us to save the computerised life from heat death on planets of other stars. Tipler does not bear in mind the eventual complete disintegration of the universe (in tens of billions of years) as the astronomers predict, either through a 'big crunch' (a collapse followed by another big-bang), or more likely through a 'big whimper' (continuous expansion leading eventually to a matterless cold photon cloud). In both cases nothing will remain of Tipler's supercomputers.

## 5.3 End of life

Given the inevitability of death, most of us prefer a rapid, painless death rather than an extended period of serious physical suffering. But a rapid death has two disadvantages: 1. One has no opportunity to prepare oneself for dying; 2. It makes it impossible to take leave of one's loved ones. A survey in the Netherlands among 1570 persons showed five styles of dealing with the final phase of life: 1. Pro-active persons (18%) arrange for their death by preparing a testament and a medical will; 2. Detached persons (22%) do not think about death; 3. Trusting persons (12%) feel supported by their faith and by loved ones; 4. Rational persons (15%) rely on medical care; 5. Social persons (33%) live without worry, denying death and in the company of friends.[6] The purpose of this survey was to provide care-givers insight in the different ways in which people approach the end of life.

## Euthanasia

Due to the advanced medical treatment possibilities, a patient often dies after a lengthy illness process with serious physical suffering. This has led to the call for euthanasia in many countries. In the Netherlands, after lengthy discussions, a law was passed in April 2001, which makes it possible for a physician to terminate the life of a patient without facing prosecution, provided the following rules have been observed by the physician:

1. has ascertained that there is a voluntary and considered request from the patient;

2. has ascertained that the patient is terminally ill with unbearable suffering;

3. has informed the patient of his/her situation and prospects;

4. has come to the agreement with the patient that in his/her situation there is no reasonable alternative;

5. has consulted at least one other independent physician, who has seen the patient and has given his judgment in writing that rules 1 - 5 have been observed;

6. has carried out the termination in a medically acceptable way.

The physician submits an extensive report to a committee of three (lawyer-chairman, physician and ethicist) appointed by the minister of health. If the committee is satisfied that all rules have been observed, no further action is taken. If not, then the report is sent to the coroner for possible legal action. After the passage of the law the Dutch Medical Society has removed from the Hippocratic oath the pledge not to administer lethal drugs.

It is clear that the ultimate decision rests with the physician and not with the patient. Soon after the passage of the euthanasia law the question was raised whether euthanasia would be permissible in (non-terminal) serious psychiatric suffering. A psychiatrist assisted in the suicide of a 51-year old woman who had lost her husband and two sons and suffered severe depression. The Dutch High Court did not convict him, but he was reprimanded by the medical disciplinary court for not letting the woman receive further treatment.

Presently, there is a discussion about the possibility of requesting euthanasia after one reaches the age of 75 and is 'ready with life'.[7] Undoubtedly the fear of getting Alzheimer's disease, when one cannot apply for euthanasia anymore, plays a role here. However, it is unlikely that this will be accepted by parliament in the foreseeable future. The requirement for 'unbearable suffering in a terminal stage' would then have to be replaced by 'lack of quality of life'. This is a very subjective judgment, which may suddenly change, e.g. through finding a new partner or a new hobby or participation in some form of volunteer activity. I agree with ethicist

Frits de Lange that it is morally unacceptable to call in the help of a physician or other person for this form of suicide.[8] Both Chabot[7] and De Lange[8] point to the possibility of refusing food and fluid, with the treating physician providing adequate palliative care.

The discussion about this form of terminating life suggests that many people are not aware anymore that life is a gift of God and that we can therefore not freely dispose of our life. For the Roman-Catholic church this is a reason to reject euthanasia and refuse a funeral service in church for someone of whom it is known that he/she has died after legal euthanasia. The Anglican Communion has also spoken out on this ground against euthanasia at the Lambeth Conference of 1998, but without calling for sanctions. The Dutch Reformed Church has also expressed a negative view of euthanasia and suggested as an alternative the possibility of palliative sedation.

### Palliative sedation

This is bringing a terminal patient in a condition of sleep for the purpose of suppressing pain and other undesirable symptoms where pain-killing medicine has insufficient effect. Since palliative sedation does not have the purpose of shortening the life of the patient, this may be considered as normal medical treatment, is thus not punishable and does not need to be reported.

The request for palliative sedation can come from the patient, but also from next of kin or nurse. In the latter case the patient must give his/her consent if able to do so. It must be made clear to patient and next of kin that they must say farewell before the beginning of sedition as the patient may not regain consciousness.

Since generally no food and fluid can be administered during sedation, life expectancy may not be more than two weeks. If the patient dies within that period, then this is due to the disease. If death occurs later, it is the result of lack of fluid and the sedation is turning into a form of euthanasia. In order to avoid this, the patient is allowed to regain consciousness by temporarily interrupting the sedation.

In the Netherlands in 2010 135,000 persons died, 1.8% of them by euthanasia and 8% after palliative sedation.

## 5.4 Conclusions and summary

Our current biomedical knowledge can explain human mortality and describe the dying process as the result of the cessation of vital functions through disease or accident. But biomedicine cannot tell us anything about life after death, only about the decomposition of the body after death. The latter knowledge permits us to formulate criteria for a responsible organ transplantation procedure.

Life expectancy has strongly increased through improved hygiene, nutrition and medical care in the past 150 years, particularly in the western countries. This positive development also has its drawbacks. Pension systems have difficulty meeting the payments to their longer-living pensioners. Therefore many countries attempt to raise the retirement age. Another problem is the rapidly increasing costs of medical care for the increasing number of elderly persons, who moreover often suffer from several chronic diseases.

The present maximum human age is 122 years, longer than most animals. There are two limiting factors, telomere loss and apoptosis. Each chromosome has a cap of 50 to 60 DNA molecules, the telomere. In each cell division the telomere loses one DNA molecule, which limits the possible number of divisions. The cell has an enzyme, telomerase, that builds up the telomeres, but it is inactive in normal adult cells. Activation of this enzyme might theoretically remove this limitation, however with a considerable risk of inducing cancer. Apoptosis (programmed cell death) removes damaged cells. It might theoretically be possible to activate apoptosis in the cells of an elderly person and thereby remove damaged cells, including cancer cells before they can cause disease. It would be a risky undertaking with moreover uncertain benefits.

Frank Tipler has described a mechanism for assuring our immortality through digital storage of humans in a future supercomputer. In order to save humanity from heat death through the conversion of the sun in a red giant, he proposes to send these computers to extragalactic planets. He forgets that eventually all stars will turn intored giants and galaxies will disappear during the expected complete disintegration of the universe.

Owing to our advanced medical technology a patient often dies only after a lengthy sickness process with severe physical suffering. The Dutch euthanasia law of 2001 offers a physician the legal possibility to terminate the life of a patient, if a number of conditions are satisfied. The number of euthanasia requests is increasing rapidly in the Netherlands and one third of the general practitioners feel pressured by patients and their relatives. Yet, in 2010 only 1.8% of deaths were the result of euthanasia. There is now a group wishing to permit euthanasia for persons over 75 who are 'ready with life'.

As Christians we should realize that life is a gift of God and thus we cannot freely dispose of our life. The major churches, Roman Catholic, Anglican and Reformed, have all come out against euthanasia.

An alternative to euthanasia is palliative sedation in which a terminal patient, who is suffering severe pain, untreatable with pain-killing drugs, is put to sleep through medication. Since the purpose is not to shorten the life of the patient, this is normal medical treatment and thus legal. Life expectancy should be less than two weeks to avoid death through deprivation of food and fluid, which would constitute euthanasia.

# Chapter 6

# Near-Death Experiences

## 6.1 The Phenomenon

About 18% of people, who after clinical death through cardiac arrest have been reanimated, report experiences. There is a general pattern that is however not always completely pursued: a feeling of peace and rest; an out-of-body experience; movement through a dark tunnel; entering a world of light; meeting a being of light (Light Person) and predeceased relatives and friends; a life review; experience of a barrier; return and awakening. It occurs in adults as well as children, in different ethnical groups, and in religious believers as well as unbelievers.

These 'near-death experiences' (NDE) were first described in 1975 by Raymond Moody, physician and philosopher[1,2] and subsequently by many others.[3-11] In 1977 the International Association for Near-Death Studies was founded with its own journal, *The Journal of Near-Death Studies.*

I shall deal in particular with the work of the Dutch cardiologist Pim van Lommel, for three reasons: 1. He was sceptical when he encountered his first case during his training as a cardiologist, then decided to set up a prospective scientific study (all patients were interviewed within five days after reanimation with a questionnaire starting with the question "Can you remember anything from the period of your cardiac arrest?"), 2. The results of his study were accepted for publication in the renowned British medical journal *The Lancet*,[12] and 3. He is not a Christian believer.

In Van Lommel's study 344 patients with 509 successful reanimations were interviewed between 1988 and 1992; 62 of them (18%) had an NDE.[13] During the NDE 56% of the 62 patients had positive emotions, 24% had an out-of-body experience, 31% experienced movement through a tunnel, 23% encountered the 'Light Being', 23% observed colours, 29% observed a 'heavenly scenery', 32% met deceased relatives or friends, 13% had a 'life review', 8% experienced a barrier from which they had to retreat.

 Comparison with the 282 patients without NDE showed no differences from the 62 patients with NDE in circumstances during the reanimation, such as duration of cardiac arrest, previous medication, in prior knowledge of NDE, or in religion and education.

Of Van Lommel's 62 NDE cases 37 people could be imterviewed again at 2 and 8 years after their reanimation. They had a vivid remembrance of their experience. Compared with patients without NDE they had a diminished fear of death, a strengthened belief in life after death and an increased empathy for others.

Jeffrey Long collected 613 NDE cases by means of a well-designed 48-item questionnaire (that would put off most fakers) on his NEDRF website.[9] It is interesting that the percentages for the various aspects of NDE were generally higher than those reported by Van Lommel (figures in parentheses): 75.4% out-of-body experience (24%), 52.5% positive emotions (56%), 33.8% tunnel experience (31%), 57.3% % encountering a Light Being and relatives (23% and 32%), 22.2% having a life review (13%), 52.2% seeing a 'heavenly scenery' (29%), 31.0% meeting a barrier (8%).

W.C. van Dam[10] discusses NDE on the basis of the books of Moody[1,2] and Rawlings[3] (Van Lommel's study had not yet been conducted). He considers NDE in the light of the biblical teaching about what happens after death, and concludes that the NDE findings on the whole fit within the biblical context.

A somewhat different NDE has been described by psychiatrist George Ritchie.[14] In 1943 at the age of 20 he volunteered for military service. During training in Camp Barkeley, Texas, he came down with double lobar pneumonia and after cardiac arrest was pronounced dead. He experienced flying through the air from Camp Barkeley to his family in Richmond, Virginia. Because he was neither seen nor heard by anyone, he 'flew' back to the hospital in Camp Barkeley and found there his 'dead' body. At that moment Christ appeared to him as the Light Being, who asked him what he had done with his life. Ritchie then had a life review. Actually, after he had been pronounced dead, he was in coma, from which he spontaneously regained consciousness after four days. Interestingly, he experienced existing in a non-material body like the resurrection body of Christ: passers-by walked right through his body and when he tried to grasp a lantern pole, his hand passed straight through it.

## 6.2 Is NDE an artefact?

Sceptics maintain that NDE is a neurophysiological arte-fact due to the effects of cardiac arrest and brain death. Moody already considered this possibility in his first book: oxygen deprivation in the brain, hallucinations from med-ication, neuropathological attacks, sensory deprivation, wish-fulfilling dreams.[1] He concludes that none of these possibilities can explain all cases of NDE and certainly not the full NDE pattern. Rawlings finds that patients who receive hallucinogenic medication or suffer diseases causing hallucinations, such as uremia or schizophrenia, actually have a lower incidence of NDE.[3]

Peter and Elizabeth Fenwick note that the religious background of the patient has no effect on the obser-vation of a Light Person and that for most persons the NDE has a lasting transforming effect on their sub-sequent life.[6] They feel that these findings speak against the idea that NDE is a neurophysiological artefact.

Mark Fox devotes 64 pages in his book to a review of all attempts to explain NDE as an artefact and concludes that not a single one of these can explain the full NDE, particularly the vivid memory and the life-transform-ing effect.[8] He describes cases of blind persons with a NDE who report seeing details during their out-of-body experience (the first stage of NDE) they could never have 'seen'. One might call this 'transcendental vision'.

Van Lommel also devotes extensive attention to the question whether NDE may be an artefact.[15] He notes that the mere fact that only 18% of all reanimated per-sons in his study report a NDE pleads against an arte-factual basis.[10] He says that initially he was convinced that cerebral hypoxia (lack of oxygen in the brain) caused the NDE. However, hypoxia caused by low blood pressure, cardiac failure or oppression leads to unrest, confusion and agitated behaviour, but never NDE. In a threatening accident or a depression NDE can occur without hypoxia. Hypercarbia (high $CO_2$ level in blood) is known to cause in some persons certain aspects of NDE, such as out-of-body experience, tunnel experience, a feeling of peace, brief flashes of memory, but not a life review or encounters with deceased persons. In a study of $CO_2$ levels in exhaled breath after successful reanimation it was found that the higher the $CO_2$ level the more frequently NDE was reported but of the 52 patients in this study only 21% reported NDE.[16]

Psychologist Susan Blackmore claims that hypoxia in the eye could explain the tunnel experience in NDE.[17] However, the feeling of high speed in the tunnel and the encounter with predeceased relatives and friends can hardly be ascribed to ocular hypoxia.

Ketamine, which in the past was used as a narcotic, causes sometimes in low dosage out-of-body and tunnel experiences but no life review or encounters with predeceased friends. Moreover, ketamine-like substances have never been found in the body or the brain. So ketamine can also be excluded as a cause of NDE.

Endorphin, a morphine-like substance, is released during stress and can then abolish pain and cause a feeling of peace and well-being. Susan Blackmore therefore attributes NDE to the release of endorphine.[17] But, says Van Lommel, the action of endorphin usually lasts some hours, whereas the absence of pain and the feeling of peace accompanying NDE quickly disappear after regaining consciousness following reanimation.

It has often been claimed that NDE is a hallucination, such as occurs in schizophrenia, psychosis or excessive drug use. However, persons with NDE are generally emotionally stable and have not used alcohol or drugs. Furthermore, hallucinations differ from person to person, while NDE reports show a rather common pattern. A hallucination is an observation that has no basis in reality, while during NDE verifiable observations occur, such as the location of a patient's lost denture or a tennis shoe on a hospital window ledge.

Carl Sagan, renowned astronomer and atheist, ascribed NDE to a reliving of the birth process.[18] The dark tunnel would then be the uterus and at the emergence from it the light would appear. However, a newborn does not yet see anything at that point and does not have the capacity to memorize the birth process and remember it.

Sceptic Michael Shermer thinks that the problem has been solved: electrical stimulation of the right temporal lobe causes out-of-body experiences, so "a part of the brain causes these illusions (NDE), another part then interprets them as external events".[19] He doesn't consider the possibility that stimulation of the temporal lobe might produce the same neuronal processes as occur during cardiac arrest and NDE. Moreover, NDE occurs largely after brain death has set in and neuronal activity has ceased.

It is interesting that the atheist philosopher Alfred J. Ayer ((1910-1998) related in an article "What I saw when I was dead", appearing shortly before his death, that he had an NDE: "I was confronted by a red light, exceedingly bright, and also very painful even when I turned away from it. I was aware that this light was responsible for the government of the universe."[20] To his attending physician he would have said that he saw a divine being and that he was afraid he would have to revise his opinions and his books.

On the basis of all these arguments Van Lommel concludes that NDE is a reality that cannot be dismissed as an artefact due to the physical conditions resulting from cardiac arrest and reanimation. This is also my conclusion.

## 6.3 Van Lommel's explanation of NDE

If NDE is not an artefact, says Van Lommel, then there remains the cardinal question: "How can a clear consciousness outside of our body be experienced when the brain no longer functions during a period of clinical death with a flat EEG (electroencephalogram)?" [13] Changes in the EEG begin 6.5 sec after the onset of cardiac arrest and after 15 sec the EEG is flat, indicating that brain death has begun. This means that the major part of the NDE occurs when brain function has ceased. After 37 sec of cardiac arrest it may take hours to days after reanimation before the EEG has returned to normal. We must therefore find an explanation for the existence of a clear consciousness during a period of brain death.

Van Lommel attempts to answer this question by means of quantum theory.[21] He thinks that our mind (he uses the word 'consciousness' but this is the functioning of the mind) is located outside the body, under normal conditions as well as during brain death after cardiac arrest. He postulates that the mind is connected to the brain by means of quantum mechanical 'entanglement'. The latter is the phenomenon that two photons or electrons, released from a single source, continue to influence each other, e.g. in their spin condition (spin is the rotation of an elementary particle). The influencing would occur through the exchange of 'quantum information', even at distances of many miles. According to Van Lommel, the mind is located outside the body during life and is connected to the brain through entanglement. During brain death, if I understand Van Lommel correctly, the entanglement would be broken and during reanimation it would be restored.

I see two problems with this hypothesis. First, quantum theory is valid only at the level of elementary particles, but not at the level of our body organs. Van Lommel attempts to overcome this problem but not in a convincing manner.[22] Secondly, entanglement of elementary particles is very fragile. Merely influencing one of the particles, e.g., by observation, breaks the entanglement; in laboratory experiments within a microsecond.[23] Only at – 270 ºC, close to absolute zero, entanglement is retained in a crystalline material.[23] Communication between an extracorporeal mind and the brain via entanglement would thus be continually under the threat of being broken. A scientific explanation of NDE is difficult because we here appear to be crossing the border between the biological and the transcendental worlds and thus experimental studies would hardly seem possible. Rejecting Van Lommel's hypothesis, however, does not detract in any way from the veracity of his findings about NDE.

## 6.4 An alternative explanation of NDE

First I would like to retain the notion of the unity of body and mind during *life*, as taught by the Old and New Testaments (chs. 2 and 3) and confirmed by our current neurophysiological insights. In living humans the mind is capable of collecting, processing and storing information and also of communicating this informa- tion to others. The neuronal networks in the brain serve as the biological substrate for these functions without the mind being a part of the brain. Reductionists like Dick Swaab,[25] who believe that the mind is part of or even identical to the brain, get into difficulties with a mind that is still functioning during brain death.

During NDE the neuronal networks in the brain no longer function, as indicated by a flat EEG. The patient can still see and hear, and can process and store the observations but is incapable of communicating them to others. Only after successful reanimation with restoration of the brain function can the person with a NDE communicate this experience to others. Functioning neuronal networks are thus an absolute requirement for communication only.

This leads me to the conclusion that, after cardiac ar- rest during NDE, the unity of body and mind is lost and the mind leaves the body. The mind can then no longer communicate with other persons, but remains functioning in observing the environment, its earthly surroundings during the first few moments, and later after passage through the tunnel seeing a transcendent 'heavenly' scenery. During a successful reanimation the mind is pulled back into the body and then regains the ability to communicate.

It seems reasonable to assume that when reanimation is unsuccessful and the patient dies, the mind remains separated from the body which begins to decay. The mind then exists in the interim period between death and resurrection, which is discussed in the next chap- ter. In contrast to Van Lommel, I maintain the unity of body and mind during life and I do not invoke a quantum mechanical 'entanglement' between body and mind. I conclude that at death the mind leaves the body and survives. I suggest that NDE is the account of a brief visit to the realm of the dead in a transcendent world.

## 6.5 Conclusions and summary

Patients, who have been reanimated after cardiac arrest, subsequently report in many cases having extraordinary experiences during the period of clinical death. These so-called 'near-death experiences' (NDE) show a common pattern: feelings of peace and rest, out-of-body experience, movement through a dark tunnel, emergence into a world of light, encounter with a Light Being and/or predeceased relatives and friends, a life review, meeting a barrier and return to their body. Not every person reports all of these items.

NDE has first been described in 1975 by the physician Raymond Moody, subsequently by many others. The Dutch cardiologist Pim van Lommel conducted a prospective study, which means that he and his co-workers interviewed every patient within five days of their successful reanimation by means of a fixed questionnaire. Of 344 patients 62 (18%) reported a NDE.

Could NDE be a neurophysiological artefact caused by cardiac arrest and ensuing brain death? Sceptics have put forth many possibilities: hypoxia (lack of oxygen), high $CO_2$ level in the brain, hypoxia in the eyes, hallucinations through illness or drug use, effects of ketamine-like substances or endorphin secretion, reliving the birth process, stimulation of the right parietal lobe. These effects can either be excluded or they can explain only a few of the phenomena reported by those having a NDE. With Van Lommel I conclude NDE is a reality and not an artefact.

Now the question is: How can a clear consciousness exist during a period of brain death (flat electroencephalogram)? Van Lommel attempts to answer this question by assuming a quantum mechanical entanglement between an extracorporeal mind and the brain. During brain death the entanglement would be broken, but after reanimation it would be restored. My objections to this hypothesis are twofold: 1. Quantum mechanical behaviour occurs at the level of elementary particles, but not at the level of the brain; 2. Entanglement between two particles is a very unstable condition. It is broken within a microsecond upon mere observation of one of the particles; only at a temperature near absolute zero does it become stable. Communication between an extracorporeal mind and the brain via entanglement would be constantly at risk of being disrupted.

A scientific explanation of NDE is hardly possible because here we appear to cross the threshold between the biological and transcendental worlds and experimental studies are difficult or impossible.

For an alternative explanation of NDE I proceed from the biblical image of the body-mind unity during life, which is confirmed by our current neurophysiological insights. The mind is capable of collecting, processing and storing information, and also of communicating this information to others. The neuronal networks in the brain serve as the biological substrate for these functions of the mind, but without mind and brain being identical. During brain death following cardiac arrest the functioning of the neuronal networks has ceased. As we notice from the NDE reports, the patient is still capable of seeing and hearing, of processing and storing his observations, but is incapable of communicating them. The patient experiences this as an out-of-body movement of the mind. During the first few moments the mind can observe the hospital room and the reanimation activities, later (after passage through the tunnel) it can observe the abode of the dead and what happens there. Only after a successful reanimation, with restoration of brain functioning, the mind reenters the body and the patient can communicate the NDE experiences to others.

After a failed reanimation, the mind cannot return to the dead body and exists in the interim period between death and resurrection, which is the subject of discussion in the next chapter.

# Chapter 7

# The Interim Period

## 7.1 Biblical data

By the interim period I mean the period between our death and the resurrection of all the dead on the last day. The Bible does not tell us much about this period, apparently for the simple reason that the return of Christ was expected by the disciples within their lifetime, by Paul (1Thess.5:1-11), by the author of the first letter of Peter (1Pet.4:7), and even by Jesus himself (Mk.9:1).

Actually, there are only three texts that might possibly refer to the interim period: 1Thess.4:15; Lk.16:19-31; 1Pet.3:19. In 1Thess.4:15 Paul speaks about *"those who have fallen asleep"* (RSV, 1953), which led to the common belief that during the interim period the dead are asleep. Hence the words 'rest in peace' on numerous tombstones and the hymn 'requiescat in pace' in the Latin funeral mass. However, the Greek verb *koimao* used by Paul literally means 'to fall asleep'. It refers not so much to the condition of the dead during the interim period as to the dying process. The newer NRSV translation (1995) simply has *"those who have died"*.

In Lk.16:19-31 we read the story of the poor Lazarus and the rich man. Both die: Lazarus is *"carried away by the angels to be with Abraham"*, while the rich man goes to Hades, the abode of the dead, *"where he was being tormented"*. Far away he sees Abraham with Lazarus by his side and begs him to send Lazarus to bring him relief. Abraham replies: You had your good things during your lifetime and Lazarus only had misery. Now the situation has been turned around. Moreover, there is great chasm fixed between you and us, so nobody from here can come to you. Then the rich man thinks of his five brothers who are still alive. He asks Abraham to send Lazarus to his brothers to warn them. This request is also turned down by Abraham, who says: they have Moses and the prophets (the Torah, the Jewish Bible). The rich man says: if somebody from the dead comes to them, they will certainly repent. Abraham remains adamant: if they will not listen to Moses and the prophets, neither will they be convinced if someone rises from the dead. This parable told by Jesus expresses the idea that the dead do not sleep peacefully, but that they will either suffer or have a good time, depending on their behaviour during their earthly life. However, it will be clear that Jesus did not tell this parable to teach his followers about the interim period, but to warn them of the consequences of their behaviour on earth. Who lives in wealth, without caring about the poor at his doorstep, will later receive his retribution.

The author of the first letter of Peter writes: *in which also he* (Jesus) *went and made a proclamation to the spirits in prison* (1Pet.3:19). He is speaking here about the contemporaries of Noah. In Jn.10:16 Jesus says: *I have other sheep that do not belong to this fold* (those who are not Jews). *I must bring them also, and they will listen to my voice.*

For the place where the dead remain four words are used in the Bible: *Sheol, Hades, Gehenna* (Hell) and *Paradise*. Hades is the Greek translation of the Hebrew word Sheol, which is for the Jews the place where the minds of the dead sojourn, waiting for the last judgment. It was not seen as a place of torment, although a bad conscience leading to fear for the coming judgment might make it such. Where in the Apostles' Creed it says that Jesus after the crucifixion *'descended into hell'*, this means that he visited the dead in Hades, presumably to prepare them for taking part in the resurrection of all dead at the return of Christ. Gehenna is a Greek word derived from Hinnom, a valley south of Jerusalem, where during the monarchy an idolatrous cult burnt children as an offering to the gods; it is therefore the equivalent of a fiery hell.

Paradise stems from the Persian word for a walled garden. As such it is used in the Septuagint (the Greek translation of the Old Testament) for the Garden of Eden where Adam and Eve were placed (Gen.2:8). Gradually, 'Paradise' came to be seen as the abode of the blessed minds. In this sense Jesus uses the word in his promise to the repentant criminal who was crucified with him: *'today you will be with me in Paradise'* (Lk. 23:43).

In view of the phrase in the Apostles' Creed, this means that we should not see Hell, Hades and Paradise as really different places. We humans seem to have an irrepressible desire to make a distinction between a place for the 'good' and one for the 'bad' among the dead, for Paradise and Hell. We noticed this already in the discussion of the ancient religions in chapter 1. What is neglected then is that a last judgment loses its meaning: it would mean that the distinction has already been made upon the entrance to the realm of the dead. Therefore, I use the neutral term 'realm of the dead', where the minds of the dead spend the time between death and resurrection.

## 7.2 Further biblical considerations

In the context of NDE the Dutch theologian W.C. van Dam discusses other Bible texts that make reference to a life after death.[1] He mentions Ps.88:10,12 *(I am counted among those who go down to the Pit* [Sheol]; *I am like those who have no help. Are your wonders known in the darkness, or your saving help in the land of forgetfulness?)* as representing the original Jewish thinking that those who die will dwell in Sheol abandoned by God. Gradually there arose the belief in God's care for those in Sheol, as in Ps.73:24 *(You guide me with your counsel, and afterwards you will receive me with honour).* A belief in a resurrection is expressed late in the Old Testament by the prophet Daniel who says: *Many of those who sleep in the dust of the earth shall awake, some to everlasting life, and some to shame and everlasting contempt* (Dan.12:2). In Mt.13:41-43, 49-50 Jesus speaks about purgatory for the evildoers, but without labelling this as an interim period. But in Mt. 25:41 Jesus speaks about the 'eternal fire' for those who have neglected their neighbours, while the righteous will receive eternal life. Paul speaks about the last judgment (2Cor. 5:10), but also without mentioning an interim period. Death with an immediate judgment is concisely posed in the letter to the Hebrews: *... just as* *it is appointed for mortals to die once, and after that the judgment.* (Heb.9:27).

In Eph.5:14 Paul seems to speak about a state of sleep *(Sleeper, awake! Rise from the dead…)*, but in Phil.1:23 he doesn't seem to recognize an interim period *(my desire is to depart and be with Christ)*.

On the other hand, there is also the thought that the dead who will be raised are already alive. This is suggested by Jesus' reference to the story of the burning bush (Ex.3:2-6): *'…the fact that the dead are raised Moses himself showed, in the story about the bush, where he speaks of the Lord as the God of Abraham, the God of Isaac, and the God of Jacob. Now he is God not of the dead, but of the living; for to him all are alive'* (Lk.20:37-38; also Mk.12:26-27). Jesus says to Martha: *Those who believe in me, even though they die, will live, and everyone who lives and believes in me will never die.* (Jn.11:25-26; also in Jn.3:36 and Jn.6:47).

An indication for an interim period is found in the Book of Revelation: … *I saw under the altar the souls of those who had been slaughtered for the word of God and for the testimony they had given.* (Rev.6:9). Peter mentions that Jesus preached to the spirits in the realm of the dead (1Pet.3:19; 4:6). As mentioned in the previous section, the story of the rich man and Lazarus (Lk.16:19-31) offers a glimpse of the interim period, but it is a parable from which we may not draw far-reaching conclusions.

The 'Light Person', who is often observed within NDE, recalls places in the gospel of John where Jesus is called 'the light of the world' (Jn.1:9; 12:35). The world of light that is reached from the dark tunnel during NDE, reminds us of the city of light in Rev.21:23 and 22:5.

In conclusion we may state that although the Bible offers suggestions of an interim period in several places, it nowhere gives a clear picture of it. This is probably due to the expectation of Jesus and his Apostles that the return of Christ would occur within their generation. In Jn.21:20-23 Jesus says that his disciple John might remain alive until that day. In the meantime we live 2000 years later and are still awaiting the return of Christ. Every reason therefore to do some more thinking about the interim period.

## 7.3 What other theologians say about the interim period

On the one hand, we have the biblical teaching of the unity of body and mind. On the other hand, there is the ancient Greek belief in an immortal soul that during life is locked up in a mortal body, but at death is liberated and lives eternally. The Greek belief has been rejected by the Church from early on.

Klaus Berger holds so strongly to the biblical teaching of the body-mind unity that he assumes that at death the mind dies with the body and will come to life again in the resurrection body at the return of Christ.[2] He does not speak about NDE and what might be derived from it about the condition of the mind during the interim period. What remains according to Berger is a 'name' in the biblical sense of the word, as a symbol of the identity of the person during life and after death. This identity would exist for every person individually in relation to God. Berger refers to Isa.43:1, where God says to Jacob: ..., *I have called you by name, you are mine.* And to Lk.10:20 where Jesus says to his disciples: ... *rejoice that your names are written in heaven.*

Whoever knows the name of a person, says Berger, has the power to either bless or curse this person. Although Berger devotes 54 pages to his 'name' idea, he does not succeed in explaining what having a name before God can tell us about the interim period. Having a name before God means that God knows us as an individual creature from birth to death and subsequently to the resurrection at the return of the Son. Very important, but it doesn't tell us anything about what happens to us during the interim period.

Keith Ward holds to a separate existence of the mind during the interim period: "Consciousness of some sort could exist without material embodiment, but it might be very unlike present human consciousness … The decay and death of the brain need not destroy consciousness, though it impairs the exercise of conscious abilities." [4] As Ward doesn't speak about NDE at all, he remains rather vague about the state of the mind during the interim period.

Dinesh D'Souza, in his book *"Life after Death, The Evidence"* (2009), mentions the interim period only on the basis of the resurrection of Christ.[5] He mentions NDE briefly, saying that this can be only an indication of a survival of consciousness but that it shows us little about the nature of survival. It seems to me that he has not really studied the NDE literature sufficiently.

Wim Weren devotes a few lines in the last chapter his book on the afterlife to NDE, but he rejects it on account of Van Lommel's hypothesis that the mind would also function outside the body during life.[6] One can, however, reject this hypothesis (as I do) without invalidating the reality of NDE (ch.6.3). Weren remains silent on the subject of the interim period.

Guido Derksen et al. describe the development of Christian thinking about heaven and hell in humorous fashion (representing it in a fictitious metro map drawn by Jop Mijwaard), but they remain silent on the interim period as such.[7]

Harmen de Vries devotes an extensive, scholarly Bible study to the question how the dead will be resurrected.[8] Only in the last four pages of his 350-page book – as if it were an afterthought or acceding to the publisher's request – he considers the question whether we shall meet loved ones in the hereafter; his answer is that this is a reasonable assumption. Only at this point does De Vries allude to a 'possible interim' between death and resurrection. About NDE he doesn't speak at all.

## 7.4 What we can learn from near-death experiences

In ch. 6 I have concluded that NDE is not a neurophysiological artefact due to the effects of cardiac arrest, and that there is thus a good reason to consider NDE as a reality. It would then offer us a glimpse of the interim period. I have argued that during NDE the mind is separated from the body-mind unity existing during life. In its independent state the mind can still see and hear, and process and store its observations, but it cannot communicate these with earthly persons. That is only possible again after successful reanimation, when the mind has returned to the body and can make use of the neuronal networks in the brain.

If reanimation fails, then the temporary situation of the mind during NDE becomes in my opinion a permanent one for the entire interim period between death and resurrection. There is no reason stubbornly to maintain

the body-mind unity after death, as Berger does.[2] After all, the biblical texts and neuroscientific data from
which we derive the body-mind unity refer to the living
person. According to Berger's claim that both body and
mind die and there remains only a name until resurrection will occur. This reduces the interim period to
a merely passive period, a data bank of names.

The life review experienced by many during NDE can
be seen as a self-judgment, in which we observe our
good and bad actions during our life time. I see this
as the starting point of a learning process of the mind
during our stay in the 'realm of light'. An argument for
assuming such a learning process is the finding that
most persons after a NDE report a changed attitude
to life in their subsequent years of life: a decreased
fear of death, a strengthened belief in life after death,
increased religious feelings (though less churchly), a
more positive attitude to life, and increased empathy
for others.[3] There is thus a long-lasting remembrance
of the NDE with drastic consequences for later life.
This suggests to me that during the interim period
our mind is growing from its earthly level to the level
required for eternity life in the future world. Thus the
life review is not a 'last judgment', but a self-judgment
that gives direction to a further growth of our mind
during the interim period.

The interim period serving as an opportunity for spiritual growth is confirmed by the NDE of children.[9] A
five-year old child had a NDE during a coma due to
meningitis. When she awoke from the coma, she reported that she had been addressed in the 'realm of
light' by an approximately 10-year old girl. This girl
told her that she was her sister Rietje and that she had
died a month after her birth. The parents confirmed

that they had indeed had a baby whom they had called Rietje and who had died at this early age. It is striking that Rietje did not appear as a baby but as a 10-year old girl. Apparently, there is during the interim period not only a spiritual growth but also an aging process in the case of those who died at a very early age.

Now there arises the question as to where the mind resides during the interim period. On account of the NDE reports this would be a 'realm of light', where the minds of the dead reside in an active state. Deceased relatives and friends are met and recognized during the NDE and communication with them is possible, at least to a certain extent. This is quite different from the Old Testament *Sheol* where the dead sleep (Jer.51:39, 57), but abandoned by God (Ps.88:10,12). Neither is it 'heaven', for this the place where God the Father resides (Mt.5:16; 6:1, 9; Mk. 11:26; Lk.11: 13; Jn.3:31) and of which the new kingdom will be a part. Nor is it 'hell' as the site of unquenchable (Mk.9:43), eternal (Mt.18:8) fire and eternal punishment (Mt.25: 46). Entrance to either heaven or hell depends on a 'last judgment' that is supposed to occur only after the return of Christ on the last day of this world (Mt.25:31-46; Jn.5:22, 27-29). The 'realm of light' described in the NDE reports resembles more the paradise, about which Jesus speaks when he says that the repentant criminal who is crucified with him will reside there with him (Lk.23:43). I disagree with Berger who believes that paradise is the new kingdom, probably because he assumes that after our death our mind dies with the body and only a 'name' remains (section 7.3).[10] There would be no interim period and no residence for the minds of the dead, only a heavenly databank for storing the names.

What we have learned from the NDE reports also suggests an answer to the frequently raised question: What happens to those who during their life on earth have not known Jesus Christ, either because they grew up in another religion, or because they grew up in our secularized western countries where they never came into contact with the Christian church and its teachings. The 'Light Person', who is seen by many during a NDE, is recognized by the Christians among them as the Christ. It thus seems plausible that during the interim period we shall meet Christ and that he will play a key role in our learning process, as becomes clear in the NDE experience of George Ritchie.[11] So those who did not come to know Christ, or did not want to know him during their earthly life, will receive an opportunity to acquire the faith in Christ that will give them entrance to eternity life in the new kingdom.

The picture of the interim period that I have sketched here, shows that it is not a lengthy sleep, but an active learning process in preparation for what will come thereafter, eternity life in the new kingdom.

Everything I have concluded about the interim period between our death and the resurrection of all the dead after Christ's return is based on the following assumptions: 1. NDE is a reality and not a neurophysiological artefact; 2. During a NDE the mind is released from the brain-dead body and enters the realm of the dead for a brief period; 3. NDE thus offers us — in the absence of conclusive biblical information (but not incompatible with it) — a picture of what is awaiting us during the interim period.

## 7.5 Conclusions and summary

The interim period is the period between death and the resurrection of all the dead at the return of Christ. The Bible hardly speaks about this, probably because the return of Christ was expected in the lifetime of the biblical authors.

The Jews believed that the dead go the realm of the dead (Hebr. *Sheol*, Gr. *Hades*). Initially this was seen as an endless existence where the voice of God could not be heard. Later it was seen as a waiting for the resurrection and a final judgment. As in the Apostles' Creed it is said that after the crucifixion Jesus 'descended into hell' (modern text: 'descended to the dead'), then this means that he visited the dead in Hades, apparently to prepare them for the resurrection on the last day (1Pet.3:19, 4:6).

Besides *Sheol* and *Hades* the word *Paradise* is mentioned in some places. This word stems from the Persian word for a walled garden. This word gradually acquired the meaning of the abode of the blessed spirits. In this sense Jesus used it in his promise to the repentant criminal who was crucified with him. In view of the phrase in the Apostles' Creed, this means that Hades and Paradise are not really different places. But through the centuries and in different religions mankind has wanted to make a distinction between a place for the 'good' and for the 'bad'. However, the last judgment would then be meaningless; the distinction would already have been made at the entrance to the interim period. Neither is heaven the realm of the dead, because this is the place where God the Father resides. Nor is it the 'hell' as the place of eternal punishment.

Several biblical texts suggest a life after death, first for the people Israel (Ps.88), later also for individuals (Ps.73). There is also the thought that those who died are alive (Jesus referring in Lk.20:37-38 to Ex.3:2-6). The 'Light Person', often observed in NDE, reminds us of John calling Jesus 'the light of the world' (Jn.1:9; 12:35). The world of light that is seen upon emerging from the dark tunnel in a NDE, reminds us of the new Jerusalem as the city of light in Rev.21:23 and 22:5.

Few theologians speak about the interim period. Klaus Berger does, but he holds so strongly to the unity of body and mind that he believes that the mind dies with the body and will only come alive again in the resurrection body upon the return of Christ. During the interim period all that remains of a deceased person is a 'name' known to God. This makes the interim period rather meaningless. Dinesh D'Souza relates his view of the interim period entirely to the resurrection of Christ. About NDE he says that this can be an indication for a survival of the mind, but that it tells us little about the nature of survival. Wim Weren devotes a few lines to NDE, rejecting it on the basis of Van Lommel's quantum entanglement hypothesis. Rejection of this hypothesis does not, however, invalidate the reality of NDE.

If we accept that NDE cannot be adequately explained as an artefact due to the physical condition after cardiac arrest, then we have to recognize it as a reality. We can then consider a NDE as the beginning of the interim period, which is broken off by a successful reanimation.

I conclude that, upon the occurrence of brain death due to cardiac arrest, the mind is released from the brain. The free mind can still observe, process and store its observations, but cannot communicate these to living persons. This is only possible after re-entry of the spirit into the body upon a successful reanimation. The movement through the 'dark tunnel' appears to represent the passage of the mind from this world to the realm of the dead. The latter is represented as the 'world of light' in the NDE reports. There it is apparently possible to encounter predeceased relatives and friends. The 'Light Person' would be Christ who according to some biblical texts visits the dead and addresses them. The 'life review' can be seen as a self-judgment that gives direction to the learning process to be pursued during the interim period. During this learning process the mind grows from its earthly level to that required for eternity life in the future world. Even the brief stay in the interim world during NDE already is found to have deep and lasting effects on life in this world after reanimation.

# Chapter 8

# Resurrection and Eternity Life

## 8.1 Biblical data

Having made a case for a meaningful interim period from the NDE information and the scarce biblical data, we now turn to the end, the eschatology (teaching about the last things). This is the completion and perfection of the creation that is still in progress (Mk.13:19: *... from the beginning of creation that God created until now ...*; Jn.5:17: *My Father is still working, and I also am working*) There is no lack of biblical material on eschatology, which will be discussed under the headings: future, return of Christ, resurrection, judgment, eternity life.

### Future

The central message of Jesus during his earthly ministry is the coming of the kingdom of God (Mk.1:15: *The time is fulfilled, and the kingdom of God has come near ...*). Apparently Jesus expected this to happen in the near future (*Truly I tell you, there are some standing here who will not taste death until they see that the kingdom of God has come with power;* Mk.9:1). But elsewhere he says: *But about that day or hour no one knows, neither the angels in heaven, nor the Son, but only the Father;* Mk.13:32). We may see the new kingdom as the fulfilment of the creation. Jesus ascribes the new kingdom to God's action, as the present creation is also the work of God. Possibly some still doubted the creation as the work of God, but in the new kingdom God's glory will be visible to everyone.

The transformation of the present world to the new kingdom will be preceded and accompanied by a difficult time for those still alive, the apocalyptic time. This is described in Mt.24:4-51), where Jesus speaks about false messiahs, wars and threats of war, famines and earthquakes as only the birth pangs of the new kingdom. Then there will be persecutions of his followers, many will fall away and betray others, false prophets will arise. But anyone who endures to the end will be saved. Immediately thereafter sun and moon will be darkened, stars will fall from heaven, and the powers of heaven will be shaken. In Lk.17:22-37 Jesus compares all this to Noah's flood and the destruction of Sodom. It is useful to compare these predictions about the end time with elements of our present time, such as earthquakes, tsunamis, climate change, terrorism, drug abuse. Many see in these disasters an indication of apocalyptic events. This leads to frequent predictions of the last day, although these have never come true so far. However, Jesus urges us to be watchful every day.

## Return of Christ

The return of Christ (Gk. *parousia*) is predicted in many places in the New Testament: by Matthew (Mt.25:31), by Mark (Mk.13:26), by Luke (Acts 1:11); by John (Jn.14:3); by Paul who speaks about the day of the Lord (2Thess. 2:2; 1Cor.1:8, 5:5; 2Cor.1:14; Phil.1:6, 10, 2:16) and in Revelation (Rev.22:7, 20). Jesus says that he will come with the speed of lightning (Mt.24:27: *For as the lightning comes from the east and flashes as far as the west, so will be the coming of the Son of Man;* also Lk.17:24). It will be sudden and unexpected (Mt.24:37-44; Lk.17:26-35) and therefore we must always be ready (Mt.24:44, 25:13). As I said before, the time is not known to Jesus, only the Father knows it. Then Jesus will be given all power in heaven and on earth, as he said to his disciples (Mt.28:18). We may assume that this means that the Logos (the mighty Word of God) incarnate in Jesus will provide the energy needed for the transformation of the present world into the new kingdom, as the Logos did in the initial creation (Gen.1; Jn.1:1-3).

The return of Christ, the *parousia*, brings his permanent, blessed presence in the fulfilment of the history of mankind and the world. He will then be presented in his full glory (Mt.25:31). The resurrection and ascension of Christ and the sending of the Holy Spirit are the beginning of an irreversible process in which the history of salvation of mankind, and of every individual, is being fulfilled.

## Resurrection

The Old Testament has a clear expectation of the resurrection of the dead only in the book of Daniel (*Many of those who sleep in the dust of the earth shall awake, some to everlasting life, and some to shame and ever-lasting contempt;* Dan.12:2). The passage in Isaiah (*Your dead shall live, their corpses shall rise;* Isa.26:19) must be seen as the hope for the resurrection of the people of Israel after the Babylonian exile. The same can be claimed for Ezekiel 37, the resurrection of the bones in the valley.

Only in the intertestamentary writings do we find a clear message of the resurrection of the righteous dead (Enoch 91-104; Baruch 50:1ff a.o.). Enoch 1-36 and 2Macc.7 have a bodily resurrection, Enoch 91-104 a resurrection of the mind.

In the New Testament the belief in the resurrection of the dead arose before the resurrection of Christ took place (Mk.12:24-27; Mt.22:23-32; Lk.20:27-38). A bodily resurrection is assumed by Matthew, a spiritual resurrection by Mark. Paul sees the resurrection of Christ as a guarantee for the future resurrection of all the dead (Rom.8:11; 1Cor.6:14, 15:20-23; 2Cor.4:14; 1Thess. 4:14), although he fails to recognize that the resurrection of the Son of God must be seen as a unique event: the divine cannot remain in the throes of death.

The belief that we now already share in the life of the risen Christ may count as the promise of our future resurrection (Jn.11:25-26; Rom.8:11; 2Cor.1:21-22, 3:18). The completion of our transformation into the image of Christ is characterized by Paul in terms of imperishability, glory and power (1Cor. 15:42-44). The resurrection body is for Paul not like the earthly body but is a spiritual body (1Cor.15:44), transformed by the Spirit of the risen Christ. The continuity between our present existence and the resurrection life is the personal self, independent of our physical identity. God alone is immortal (1Tim.6:16), while humans are by nature mortal (Rom.5:12: *... just as sin came into the world through one man, and death came through sin, and so death spread to all because all have sinned;* a wrong explanation of Gen.3). Eternity life is the gift of God to humans by the resurrection of Christ, says Paul. The resurrection of humans represents their eschatological redemption. But for evil persons the resurrection leads to judgment (Jn.5:28-29; Mt.13:41-43).

## Judgment

In the New Testament there is a close link between the return of Christ and the judgment of all humans (Mt.12:36; Jn.3:19, 5:22, 29; 9:39; Jas. 2:13). In the letter to the Hebrews it is phrased very succinctly: *... just as it is appointed for mortals to die once, and after that the judgment;* Heb.9:27). The judgment expresses the holiness of God, whose moral will is to be obeyed (The angel *said in a loud voice, 'Fear God and give him glory, for the hour of his judgment has come';* Rev. 14:7). Therefore at the end all human creatures have to be judged on their observance of the divine commandments. Only those who have done so, will be admitted to the new kingdom.

In some places God is the judge (Rom.2:6; Heb.12:234:5; Rev.22:11; Heb.12:23; Jas.4:12; 1Pet.1:17; Rev. 20:11). In other places it is Christ who then acts as the executor of God's eschatological plan (Mt.16:27, 25:31; Jn.5:22, 9:39; Acts 10:42; 2Tim.4:1, 8; 1 Pet.4:5; Rev.22:12).

The fate of those who are condemned is described in crass terms in several places. They are destined to hell

(Heb. *gehinnom*), a place of eternal, unquenchable fire (Mk.9:43, 48; Mt.18:8, 25:30), of weeping and gnashing of teeth (Mt.8:12, 13:42, 50, 22:13, 25:30) and of outer darkness (Mt.8:12, 22:13, 25:30; 2 Pet.2:17, 3:7; Jud.13). There body and mind are destroyed (Mt.10:28). We should consider these terms as metaphors of the lasting exclusion from the presence of Christ (Mt.7:23, 25:41; 2Thess.1:9).

More hopeful and encouraging are the words of James: *... mercy triumphs over judgment* (Jas.2:13). We should also consider Martin Luther's thesis that we are justified by belief (*sola fide*), based on Rom.3:28 *(... a person is justified by faith apart from works prescribed by the law)*. Belief here means belief in Christ. Over against Paul, James says: *What good is it ...if you say you have faith but do not have works?* (Jas.2:14), and *for just as the body without the spirit is dead, so faith without good works is also dead* (Jas.2:26).

Here we have encountered the major controversy of the Reformation: justification by faith alone (Rom.3:28) or by good works (Jas.2:14, 26). It has taken nearly six centuries before a commission of Lutheran and Roman Catholic theologians appointed by both churches studied the matter.[2] They brought out a *"Joint Declaration on the Doctrine of Justification"* which states that belief in Christ is required for justification, but that 'this belief may not remain without works', and that 'what precedes or follows from the free gift of belief is neither the basis of redemption, nor earns this'. The document was accepted by both churches with only a few minor comments.

What then for those who have not known Christ? Here the interim period (ch.7.4) is of great significance; during that period we may encounter Christ, also those who have not known him or not wanted to know him during their earthly life.

## Eternity life

As mentioned in ch. 3, note 6, I prefer to use the term 'eternity life' instead of the commonly used term 'eternal life'. The latter term is based on our present idea of time but then extended to infinity, which would inevitably seem to lead to boredom. 'Eternity life', on the other hand, indicates living in the eternity of the new kingdom, life that has left transiency behind and knows no limitation of time.

About the new kingdom we read: *Death will be no more; mourning and crying and pain will be no more, for the first things have passed away* (Rev.21:4). The author of Revelation describes the new kingdom as the New Jerusalem, where God will live among us, where there is no night and no lamp or sunlight is needed anymore, because God will be our light (Rev.22:5). Neither will there be a temple (or church), because God is present in our midst (Rev.21:22).

The mysterious phrase *... the sea was no more* (Rev.21:1) refers to the remaining chaos (or 'rest-chaos'), symbolized in the Old Testament as the 'sea' against which God battles (e.g.. Job 26:12, 38:8; Ps.89:9; Ps.114:3,5; Isa.50:2; Jer.5:22; Nah.1:4). The rest-chaos is left from the initial chaos, from which God created the world (Gen.1:1-2). This rest-chaos is completely removed in the transformation to the new kingdom. In my 'chaos theology' I suggest that the rest-chaos is the source of the evil in the present world, physical as well as moral evil.[3] In the new world there will be no evil anymore, as expressed in Rev.21:4.

The prophet Isaiah already presents a picture of life in the new kingdom (*He will swallow up death forever. Then the Lord will wipe away the tears from all faces, and the disgrace of his people he will take away from all the earth, ...* Isa.25:8). Paul writes about the abolishing of evil (*The God of peace will shortly crush Satan under your feet;* Rom.16:20) and of death (*The last enemy to be destroyed is death;* 1Cor.15:26; ... *Death has been swallowed up in victory;* 1Cor.15:54).

God will have full dominion over the new kingdom (... *the Lord will become king over all the earth;* Zech.14:9). Paul assumes that at the end Christ will hand over the kingdom to the Father after he has destroyed all evil (1Cor.15:24). Here we see Christ again as the executor of God's eschatological plan.

Little is said about God's other creatures, plants and animals. Paul writes: ... *the creation itself will be set free from its bondage to decay and will obtain the freedom of the glory of the children of God.* (Rom.8:21). 'The creation itself' would include all creatures distinct from us humans, so I gladly assume that we may share the new kingdom with a variety of plants and animals. In a lighter vein, we may also expect to find heavenly restaurants, considering the many remarks about a heavenly banquet (Mt.8:11; Mk.14:25; Lk.14:15-24, 22:30). But apart from these few points, we find little biblical information about eternity life. As Paul says: *What no eye has seen, nor ear heard, nor the human heart conceived, what God has prepared for those who love him these things God has revealed to us* (1Cor.2:9).

From the reports of those who had a NDE we may assume that we shall meet our relatives and friends. Those who fear that the resurrection of the dead of all times will lead to a terrific overpopulation in the new kingdom, should consider that the restrictions of space and time existing in the present world will probably not exist in the new world, where other physical laws will apply. Moreover, there will be no married life and thus no procreation (Mk.12:25; Mt.22:30; Lk.20:35).

## 8.2 Other theologians on resurrection and eternity life

Most of the theologians of the past 80 years, discussed here, fail to argue for life after death from creation theology and to consider the interim period between death and resurrection. Of those who wrote after the publications about NDE only W.C. van Dam[4] and Dinesh D'Souza[5] paid attention to these.

John Baillie, Scottish Presbyterian, in *"And the life everlasting"* (1934) rejects the materialistic belief (also that of Klaus Berger, see below) that body and mind are so closely connected that at death the mind also dies.[6] For belief in the resurrection Baillie bases himself on Paul (1Cor. 15). He sees the new life more in terms of greater depth than of greater length. The heavenly life is a state of rest, where we shall have found what we looked for on earth. Baillie ascribes the New Testament thinking about a hell to the hatred for the persecutors of the early Christians. He rejects this idea of hell because it makes evil an eternal element in the new world. Baillie believes that a judgment is already passed at the time of our death, but it only becomes effective at the return of Christ; here he neglects the interim period.

Karl Rahner (1961), prominent Romans-Catholic theologian, believes that the soul (mind) is in this life only connected to one part of the world, namely our body, and after death is released from our body and becomes part of the world as a whole.[7] After his death, the mind of Christ also adopted a pan-cosmic state, traditionally described as his descending into hell. According to Rahner, purgatory means that a wrong relation of the soul to the created order during our lifetime will be experienced as a wrong relation to nature as a whole. The resurrection on the last day is the perfect expression of the lasting relation of the risen person to the entire cosmos.

Jürgen Moltmann (1964), German protestant theologian, suggests that the entire Christian theology should be eschatological from beginning to end, with eschatology as a mere appendix.[8] Then theology becomes hope, looking and moving forward, thereby revolutionizing and transforming the present. It thus becomes a source of earthly hope, that can compete with secular progressivism, as in Marxism. God's righteousness does not only apply to the new world, but also provides a ground of existence for the present creation.

Paul Tillich (1963), German-American protestant theologian, sees the immortality of humans as their eternal presence in the divine memory.[9] Eternal is what is good in an existing object. He rejects a continuing life beyond the grave. He seems to contradict himself when he poses on the one hand that the conscious self cannot be excluded from the Eternal Life, and on the other hand that the participation of the self is not the unending continuation of a specific stream of consciousness in memory and anticipation.

Wolfhart Pannenberg (1972), prominent German protestant theologian, considers hell as being in the absence of God but knowing of God's existence.[10] After his death Jesus stayed for three days in hell, where he addressed the minds of the dead (1Pet.3:19, 4:6). Pannenberg does not draw the conclusion from this that hell is not a place of eternal punishment, but rather the place for the dead during the interim period. The last judgment he sees as making visible the individual judgment on the basis of belief in Christ of each person who dies.

H. Berkhof (1973), Dutch protestant theologian, thinks that no meaningful statements can be made about the interim period.[11] On the resurrection of the dead he follows Paul in basing it on the resurrection of Christ, without referring to the creation and without noting the difference between the Son of God and ordinary humans. By excluding thoughts about the interim period, Berkhof wrestles with the fate of those who for any reason did not come to belief in Christ. He is more confident in his statements about eternity life. Rightly he states that the new kingdom is neither a creation, nor a re-creation, but a *transformation* of the present world.

John Hick (1976), English Anglican theologian, discusses belief in survival in ancient, eastern and western religions, looking for agreements.[12] He sees the 'soul' not as an entity created and inserted by God, but as a human 'self' or 'mind'. The mind, says Hick, survives after the death of the body. He believes that during the life of each person a heavenly replica is formed from which the resurrection body is formed. The 'spiritual' resurrection body (1Cor.15:44) is for him a new celestial body, rather than a transformed earthly body. Hick believes in universal redemption, because God has created us for community with him; this leads without coercion to reconciliation with God. About reincarnation he states that this has never been a Christian belief. But then he describes reincarnation as a form of rebirth and claims that, if this would take place in another world, there would be agreement with the Christian resurrection belief. Hick believes in the existence of extrasensory perception and telepathy, but has doubts about contact with the dead through a medium. The interim period he describes in the light of the *Tibetan Book of the Dead* and thoughts of his own.

W.C. van Dam (1980), Dutch protestant theologian, includes NDE based on the books of Moody[13] and Rawlings[14] in his considerations of life after death.[4] After an extensive description of NDE, he argues why deceit of those who report NDE or causation by a neurophysiological artefact is improbable. His tentative conclusion is that after cardiac arrest the mind of the patient leaves the body and enters the hereafter for the duration of his NDE. He sees many agreements between the NDE reports and the biblical data. He doesn't cite Eph.5:14, where Paul speaks about a 'sleep' during the interim period.

Klaus Berger (1998), German protestant theologian, illustrates his thoughts with many texts from eastern orthodox funeral liturgies.[15] The mysterious idea of a 'second death' (Rev.20:6) he sees as 'keeping your soul, find your life' in their earthly life (Mk.8:35: ... *those who want to save their life will lose it ...*). Berger devotes an entire chapter to the interim period and describes it as 'resting with Abraham' (Lk.16:19-31), but he doesn't speak about NDE or any form of spiritual growth. The resurrection is for Berger the completion of the creation process and of reconciliation with God. He rejects reincarnation, both in the original eastern and in the current western versions. He also rejects universal reconciliation as unbiblical, but is referring to serious sins rather than to unbelief in Christ. He doesn't exclude an eternal hell for those who are rejected at the last judgment.

Dinesh D'Souza (2009), a best-selling non-professional theologian of Portuguese-Indian descent, published *"Life after Death, The Evidence"*.[5] The term 'evidence' is somewhat misplaced, because his arguments are mostly of a philosophical character. One of his arguments is that all religions teach a life after death, where he equates eastern reincarnation belief and the Christian belief in a bodily resurrection. Another of his arguments is that our moral awareness implies another world with a perfect moral standard. In chapter 5, entitled 'The Physics of Immortality' (but without mentioning Frank Tipler's book bearing this title), he writes about relativity theory, big-bang theory, the fine-tuning of the physical constants, and multiple universes, and suggests that these do not exclude survival after death. The biblical data about life after death are discussed only briefly in the last chapter and only with reference to the resurrection of Christ. D'Souza considers NDE as an indication that "consciousness does survive death", but he believes that NDE tells us little about the nature of survival. The latter is probably due to the fact that he leaves the interim period between the death and resurrection of the individual person entirely out of consideration. It is regrettable that throughout the book he wages a fierce battle against atheists such as Richard Dawkins and Daniel Dennett, although this does not bring his aim – proof for life after death – any closer.

Wim Weren (2010), Dutch Roman-Catholic theologian, combines biblical texts with cultural topics to discuss

aspects of death.[16] On the subject of resurrection he devotes an extensive analysis of Ezekiel 37 to finally conclude that this deals with the restoration of the people
Israel after exile rather than the resurrection of the
dead, a conclusion that exegetes had already reached a
century ago. After three chapters on the resurrection
of Christ there follows a chapter in which Weren con-
fuses the raising and the resurrection of the dead. In
the final chapter Weren mentions NDE in a few lines,
rejecting it because of Van Lommel's hypothesis that
during life the mind also functions outside of the body.
He doesn't realize that one can reject this hypothesis
without doubting NDE (see ch.6.3). About the interim
period and the relevance of creation theology Weren
remains silent. His final words are: "through death we
land not in an endless consciousness but in an endless
emptiness. … But in this emptiness we can experience
a fullness, a presence that hides itself from us and at
the same time shows itself to us." A rather hesitant
conclusion to this book!

Guido Derksen et al. (2010) describe in their *Atlas van
het Hiernamaals* [Atlas of the Hereafter] in critical
fashion the changes in the thinking about the hereafter in the churches and among theologians.[17] They
illustrate their conclusions in humorous fashion with
a metro map drawn by Jop Mijwaard. They conclude
that heaven has become depopulated and the hell has
become ever more abstract, but do not state their own
view on the subject of life after death.

Harmen de Vries (2011), Dutch protestant pastor and
theologian, offers an extensive exegesis of Old Testament, intertestamentary and New Testament writings showing the development of the belief in an
imperishable bodily existence and a transformed

creation.[18] About the interim period and NDE he remains silent.

## 8.3 Conclusions and summary

In this chapter I discuss eschatology (teaching about the last things) on the topics: future, return of Christ, resurrection, judgment and eternity life. First the relevant biblical data are considered. Emphasis is placed on the insight that this gives concerning the completion and perfection of the ongoing creation, the transformation of the present world into the new kingdom.

The future is the coming of the new kingdom, which was the central message of Jesus during his earthly ministry. It is the perfection of the creation, in which the glory of God will become visible to all of humankind. The transformation will be preceded by disasters and afflictions.

The return of Christ is the signal that the transformation is about to take place. To him the Father will give all power in heaven and on earth, making Christ the 'manager' of the transformation process. This means in my opinion that the Logos (the mighty Word of God) that is incarnate in Jesus, will effect the transformation, just as was the case in the initial creation.

The resurrection of the dead is hesitantly predicted in some late Old Testament texts, with more assurance in some intertestamentary writings, and with full conviction in the New Testament, particularly on the basis of the resurrection of Christ. Like the creation, humans will undergo a transformation, namely from the earthly body into a heavenly spiritual body. The continuity is the personal 'self', the mind. The resurrection is the eschatological redemption of humankind.

The final judgment is inextricably connected with the return of Christ. Only those who have maintained the divine commands will receive entrance to the new kingdom. Those who fail this entrance test will be condemned to hell. The lurid descriptions of life in hell, as found in the New Testament, we may consider as metaphors for an existence in the lasting absence of God. I prefer Luther's *sola fide*, the belief in Christ, as the judgment criterion, to which I return in the next and final chapter.

Eternity life knows no more death, evil and suffering. Neither will there be restrictions of space and time, so we need not fear overpopulation from the risen dead of all centuries and nations. God will be present as king, making churches and temples superfluous. About plants and animals nothing is said, but I like to believe that there will be a new ecology of humans, animals and plants, as predicted by Isaiah (Isa.11:6-8). From the NDE reports I assume that we shall meet relatives and friends in the new life.

After discussion of the biblical data I made a critical study of the thinking of thirteen theologians on life after death and summarized the crucial points. It is remarkable that none of them starts from creation theology: perfection of the creation in the transformation to the new kingdom, in which logically all creatures will participate. Another remarkable finding is that, except for John Hick and Klaus Berger, none of them speaks about the interim period. John Hick derives his thoughts about the interim period from the *Tibetan Book of the Dead*. Klaus Berger considers the interim period as resting with Abraham, but he does not speak about NDE. Nearly all those, who wrote after publication of the books of Moody and Rawling, do not mention NDE at all. Van Dam is the only one who gives much attention to NDE: he concludes that it cannot be ascribed to fraud or a neurophysiological artefact, and that there are many agreements with biblical data. D'Souza believes that NDE can tell us little about the nature of life after death except a survival of consciousness, but he neglects the interim period. Wim Weren mentions NDE in a few lines, but rejects it on account of Van Lommel's hypothesis that the mind also functions outside the body during life. However, rejection of this hypothesis does not invalidate NDE. Harmen de Vries extensively discusses the biblical development of the belief in a bodily resurrection, but remains silent about the interim period and NDE.

Over against the views of these thirteen theologians I shall present in the next and final chapter my view about life after death.

# Chapter 9

# A Novel View

## 9.1 Starting at the beginning

To answer the question about life after death and of the credibility of the Christian faith in general, it is in my opinion essential to start with creation. For most people the belief in creation to explain the origin of the cosmos and of life on earth is not all that difficult. The more so, because science can tell us a lot about the *course* of both processes but not of their *origin*.

In the creation story in Genesis 1 we read that God created through his mighty Word, *Logos* in Greek. The Logos represents God's creative energy. The Holy Spirit, who is the Communicator between God and his world, will have brought into the early cosmos the physical laws and fundamental constants that have ever since then governed the entire evolution of the cosmos and of life.

Because his human creatures have been and are disobedient to God, as described in mythical form in Gen. 3, God sent the Logos into the Jewish child Jesus of

Nazareth in order to restore the union between God and mankind. An incidental monster alliance of high priests, Pharisees, Sadducees, King Herod, Pontius Pilate and a street mob came together against the Son of God, leading to his execution. God the Father raised Jesus, because the divine cannot remain in the bonds of death. Through his teaching, death and resurrection Jesus Christ brings about the reconciliation of disobedient humankind with God.

The creation process has a beginning but also a continuation, in which God brings his creation to perfection. At that point God transforms the cosmos into the new kingdom through the action of the Logos – now incarnate in Christ. This will take place at the time of the return of Christ. All the dead will then be raised and on the basis of belief in Christ they will receive — with those still alive — eternity life in the perfected creation, the new kingdom.

In this way I have derived the chief points of the Christian faith in a logical way from the theology of creation: initial and continuing creation; christology (teaching about Christ); pneumatology (teaching about the Spirit); soteriology (teaching about reconciliation); eschatology (teaching about the last things).

I avoid the — for me — unacceptable thought that God permitted or even willed the execution of Jesus because only by sacrificing his only Son could he redeem sinful humankind. No, Jesus was executed unjustly by those who feared or hated him or those who were disappointed because he did not liberate them from Roman rule. Because Jesus was willing to undergo the depths of human life, he can effect our reconciliation with God.

## 9.2 Life after death

The question raised in this book – Is there life after death? – can in my opinion also better be answered from creation theology than from the resurrection of Jesus Christ. After all, the resurrection of Christ is a unique event, since the divine cannot remain in death. Our resurrection doesn't follow necessarily from that of Christ, since we are not divine. Paul believes that the one follows from the other (1Cor.15:12-19), although elsewhere (Acts 13:35) he seems to see the distinction when he quotes Ps.16:10 in the words: *You will not let your Holy One experience corruption.*

The creation story tells us that God created humans out of love in the course of his creative work. Then it would seem logical that God wants his human creatures to share in the perfection of his creation. This means that our mortality will be abolished and that we may participate in eternity life in the new kingdom. The resurrection of the dead seems to me to follow logically from the creation of humankind.

Human mortality is not the result of a punishment that the mythical first human pair received for their disobedience. That is not even said in Gen.3. The mortality of all living beings was essential for making the evolution of life possible; mortality is required for the operation of natural selection. Evolution of life is the way God has chosen in his wisdom for the creation of humanity and this implies the mortality of all living beings. I expect that, in the perfection of creation, evolution of life will come to an end and thus human mortality can then be lifted.

Death can therefore not be seen as an evil. At most, death becomes an evil when it is the result of human action or of a natural disaster. The dying process can in some cases involve much physical suffering, although palliative sedation can mitigate this (see ch.5). There remains the fact that the death of a loved one causes distress, even when it is the peaceful death of a person at an advanced age. However, the belief that death is not permanent and that we may meet each other again in the new kingdom, where there is no suffering and death, may provide consolation.

## 9.3 The interim period

In ch.7 I noted that the Bible hardly speaks about the interim period between death and resurrection. I attribute this to the fact that Jesus and his disciples expected the return of Christ and with it the resurrection to be imminent. In ch.8 I concluded that few theologians pay attention to the interim period, although it has already lasted up to 2000 years for those who died since the appearance of Jesus. For the place where the dead remain during this period I use the general term 'realm of the dead' in order to avoid confusion between the terms Sheol, Hades, Paradise and Heaven.

In ch.6 I studied the phenomenon of near-death experiences (NDE) after a cardiac arrest, and concluded that these cannot be explained as a neurophysiological artefact. NDE must therefore be considered as a reality that can offer us insight in the interim period. In my opinion we can see NDE as a brief stay in the realm of the dead, finished by the reanimation of the patient.

First, the mind leaves the body, in which state it can still see, hear, process and memorize observations. But it cannot communicate its observations to other persons. The 'dark tunnel' marks the transfer of the disembodied mind from the earthly world to the transcendent world of which the realm of the dead is a part. The mind observes this as entering the 'world of light' mentioned in the NDE reports. There the mind meets the 'Light Person' in whom we may recognize Christ. And in some cases predeceased relatives or friends. In a NDE the mind then feels itself drawn back to its earthly body when reanimation is successful. When reanimation fails and death ensues, it is reasonable to assume that the mind remains in the realm of the dead.

In the 'life review', reported by many persons after a NDE, one's entire preceding life is seen in a flash with all moments at which one acted wrongly. I see this as a form of self-judgment, in which we discern what we still have to learn in preparation for eternity life in the new kingdom. I suggest that our teacher is Christ, the 'Light Person', as also indicated in the first letter of Peter: ... *he went and made a proclamation to the spirits in prison.* (1Pet.3:19). With John Hick[1] I am convinced that no human reaches perfection during earthly life. On account of all this I do not believe in a two-storied realm of the dead with a lower storey for the sinners and an upper storey for the saints. Neither do I believe in a purgatory in which our sins are 'burnt off'. The thought that during the interim period we pass through a learning process geared to our individual shortcomings shows more respect of the Creator for humans whom he created in his image.

The occurrence of a NDE during brain death (15 sec after cardiac arrest) indicates that the mind survives after death. The belief in the immortality of the mind arose in the early Church, was declared a dogma by the fifth Lateran Council (1512-1517) and later adopted by Calvin and his followers. This means that the unity of body and mind existing during life is divorced at death. In some NDE reports inhabitants of the realm of the dead tell the person in NDE that they should return to earth and their body. This would mean that in the realm of the dead communication is possible, which would be desirable for the learning process during the interim period. The effectiveness of the learning process appears from the fact that most persons some years after their NDE still have a decreased fear of death, an increased belief in life after death, and an increased empathy for others, although their stay in the realm of the dead was only brief. Most of them do not speak easily about their experiences with others, apparently because they can hardly convey the depth of these experiences and are afraid of meeting with unbelief or cheap curiosity.

## 9.4 Resurrection

The interim period will be concluded with the return of Christ. Then will, according to the Bible, the resurrection of all the dead will take place. The belief in this had arisen already before the resurrection of Christ occurred, as witnessed by texts in the three synoptic gospels (Mk.12:24-27; Mt.22:23-32; Lk.20:27-38). For those still alive at the return of Christ the apocalyptic events surrounding his return will bring about an accelerated learning process, preparing them for the transition to the new life.

Paul has thought about the nature of the resurrection body (1Cor.15:35-49). He uses the analogy of a seed that, planted in the earth, dies and then brings forth a plant. This analogy is not quite right, for the seed doesn't die but undergoes a change, whereby it forms roots and a stem. Paul concludes that the earthly body decays, but that the resurrection body will be an imperishable 'spiritual' body. The stories about the appearances of the risen Christ give us an idea of his resurrection body. He can move through closed doors and can virtually appear simultaneously in different places, while he is still recognizable by his followers.

We may assume that at the resurrection the surviving mind will be united with the spiritual resurrection body, restoring the body-mind unity of the risen person. This new unity will then have at its disposal all that has been learned and experienced during earthly life as well as the interim period. In this respect I disagree with Klaus Berger, who believes that at death both body and mind die and only a 'name' remains during the interim period.[2] There can then be no learning process during the interim period, and this assumption is in contradiction with the belief in the survival of the mind from the early Church onward.

## 9.5 Judgment

Earlier I spoke about the 'life review' in NDE as a self-judgment that makes us see our wrong deeds and thoughts and probably also our weakness of faith. On the basis of what we discern in the 'life review', we can then determine the content of our learning process during the interim period. I say that we can determine the content because in the light of the realm of the dead we cannot miss or cover up anything.

In ch.8 I discussed the biblical thoughts about the last judgment. We must bear in mind that the Bible authors did not know anything about an interim period with a learning process. In that case the risen person would appear in all his earthly sinfulness before the heavenly tribunal and is either admitted to heaven, or is condemned to hell for eternity. Since we cannot undo all our sins during our earthly life, only a few of us would receive admission to heaven. We may ask and receive forgiveness for sins committed, but the next day we commit new sins or repeat the earlier ones.

Through the learning process during the interim period this vicious circle will be broken. On the one hand we will discern our past sins in the revealing light of the realm of the dead, on the other hand the temptations of the earthly life will not exist in that place. There we can grow in an upward line without the risk of falling back.

What will then be the criterion at the last judgment? Here I gladly follow Martin Luther with his *sola fide*: 'by belief alone' and this means 'belief in Christ'. Luther's claim is based on Rom.3:28 (*a person is justified by faith*) and Jn.6:47 (*whoever believes has eternal life*). It is a joyful achievement that in 1997 an official commission of Lutheran and Roman-Catholic theologians reached the agreement that belief in Christ is required for redemption, but that this belief may not remain without works,[3] so in essence Luther has been vindicated.

And I would like to see this judgment on the basis of belief in Christ also as a self-judgment. Then God does justice to humans whom he created in his image. Feigning belief in Christ in God's presence is impossible. It implies no universal salvation, as I reckon with the possibility that even after the learning process during the interim period there may be some persons who do not wish to accept belief in Christ. They force themselves to exist forever in the absence of God, which to me is 'hell'. Those who have grown up in another religion or without religion will meet Christ, the 'Light Person' (who also occurs in the NDE reports of non-Christians). They will experience him during the learning process and thus have the same chance of 'passing' the judgment as those who grew up in the Christian faith.

## 9.6 Eternity life

Life in the new kingdom will be marked by the absence of death, illness, suffering and evil. Mortality has become superfluous with the end of biological evolution. Evil, so prominently present in our current world in the form of natural disasters and disease (physical evil) and as the result of human actions (moral evil), will have been abolished.

In my 'chaos theology' (a revised creation theology)[4] I describe this as follows:

1. Initial creation from a primordial chaos as described in the two creation stories in Genesis 1 and 2;

2. Continuing creation with a remaining chaos, symbolized in the Old Testament as 'sea';

3. Evil emerges from the remaining chaos;

4. On the last day the remaining chaos is abolished (Rev.21:1: *I saw a new heaven and a new earth ... and the sea was no more*) and with it evil.

Little is said in the Bible about the other creatures, animals and plants, except for a vague indication in Rom.8:21 (*... the creation itself will be set free from its* *bondage to decay and will obtain the freedom of the children of God).* In recent years we have become aware – to our detriment and shame – of the essential importance of an ecological order of all living species for the continuity of life on earth. Therefore I gladly assume that in the new kingdom we shall also be living together with a variety of animals and plants.

From the NDE reports we may assume that we shall meet relatives and friends. According to the words of Jesus in his dispute with the Sadducees (Mt.22:30) it appears that there will be no marital relationship. It appears that we shall be living as one large family without marriage and without new births. Some people worry whether with the resurrection of all the dead from all ages the new kingdom will not become overpopulated. They should consider that the limitations of space and time of the present world will probably not exist in the new world, where a new kind of matter and different physical laws are likely to exist.

## 9.7 Eschatology and apocalypse

In eschatology (teaching about the last things) we consider the transformation of the present world into the new kingdom. Christ is the executive manager of this process (Mt.28:18). Because in him the Logos has been incarnated, I assume that the Logos will provide the energy needed for the transformation, as it also did in the initial creation. Likewise, I assume that the Spirit, as the Communicator of God, will introduce the physical laws that will give order the new kingdom. At the end of the transformation process Christ will transfer the kingship to the Father after he has abolished all evil (1Cor.15:24: *Then comes the end, when he [Christ] hands over the kingdom to God the Father, after he has destroyed every ruler and every authority and power).*

The Apocalypse is the prophetic description of the difficult times accompanying the transformation. There will be natural disasters and calamities caused by enemies and false prophets (Mt.24:4-5). That the transformation will be accompanied by such events does not seem unlikely to me, as it will be the most radical event since the beginning of creation. However, we must translate the biblical apocalyptic to the conditions in our time.

This is not so difficult since these days we experience all kinds of calamities, existing and expected. First there is the climate change as the result of our excessive and still increasing use of fossil fuels. Earlier, in 1972, there was the warning by the Club of Rome about the exhaustion of essential raw materials.[5] The oil crisis of 1973 appeared to confirm this warning, but when oil began to flow freely again the warning was soon forgotten. But now, forty years later, we are becoming aware that we have passed the peak in worldwide oil production and must rapidly search for new types of energy that will also reduce global warming. This is not so easy as some, particularly those who expect financial benefits, would have us believe. We must therefore reckon with conflicts about the shrinking oil supplies, conflicts that could assume apocalyptic dimensions, given the fact that major players possess nuclear arms. Water is a material that is also becoming scarce, particularly in S.E. Asia and African countries. Recently, the so-called 'rare earths', essential for our modern electronic equipment and batteries for electric cars, have become an issue, because China has a near-monopoly on these and is now restricting export. There also threatens to be a shortage of phosphate, an essential fertilizer.

It has already been known for over thirty years that the emission of carbon dioxide ($CO_2$) from the combustion of fossil fuels (oil, gas, coal) causes the temperature on earth to increase. The explanation is simple: the incoming sunlight consists of visible and ultraviolet radiation that is not absorbed by $CO_2$. The remaining heat is radiated by the earth as infrared radiation that is strongly absorbed by the $CO_2$ in the lower atmosphere, causing the temperature on earth to rise. This has various unfavourable consequences. Polar glaciers and sea ice melt, causing the sea level to rise and low-lying delta areas and islands to be flooded. The melting Himalayan glaciers will lead to severe water shortages in large areas of south-east Asia. Extreme weather conditions, such as cyclones, drought in some places, flooding in others, are becoming more frequent. The ecological balance between species is being disturbed, because some species adapt less well than others. This causes, for instance, shortages in fish species that serve as food. Numerous UN-sponsored conferences (Kyoto 1997; Copenhagen 2009; Cancun 2010; Durban 2011) have not led to a decrease in worldwide $CO_2$ emission.

Population increase, shortages of raw materials, food shortages for the poor, climate crisis, global economic crisis, and widespread drug abuse form the apocalypse of our time. Causes are human failure such as blindness to the facts and greed. Since these crises do not yet seem to lead to the end of humanity, I assume that this will not yet make God transform his creation. But I expect God's intervention to precede an event that would annihilate all life on earth, such as the impact of an asteroid larger than 1 kilometre or the transition of the Sun into a red giant (expected in 5 billion years' time). The occurrence of such an all-destructive event would mean that God's creation of mankind has failed. Meanwhile we shall have to endure the apocalyptic events that we have brought upon ourselves.

## 9.8 Living in expectation

We are living in the expectation of our death, the learning process during the interim period, the return of Christ with our resurrection and judgment on the criterion of our belief in Christ, followed by our transition to eternity life in the new kingdom.

What does this mean for our life here and now? It means first of all that we must shape our religious life. In my opinion that is only possible together with other faithful people in a church community. As Christians we together form a *koinonia*, a community of all who have been called by Christ. Trying to be a Christian in solitude is undesirable, because it deprives one of the sacraments and teaching of the Church and risks the loss of spiritual discipline or becoming arrogant about one's faith.

It also means that we should live in the awareness that every day could be our last one on earth. It further means that we should do our daily work to the best of our ability for the benefit of the community, that we should share in the life of our family and the wider community, that we should do whatever we can to mitigate the consequences of the apocalyptic problems of our time. In this way we may erect signs of the coming transformation of the creation by God.

## 9.9 Conclusions and summary

In order to answer the question of life after death and of the credibility of the Christian faith in general, I choose the creation as my point of departure. God created through his mighty Word, the Logos, that brings in God's creative energy. The physical laws and fundamental constants, that have governed the entire cosmic and biological evolution, were brought in by the Holy Sprit, the Communicator between God and his world. In view of man's disobedience, God sent the Logos into the Jewish child Jesus of Nazareth to repair the bond between God and humanity. Through his teaching, death and resurrection Jesus brings about the reconciliation between humanity and God. Jesus' death is the work of his human enemies (high priests, Sadducees, Pharisees, King Herod, Pontius Pilate and the mob), not of a God who can redeem humanity only by sacrificing his only Son. God will bring the continuing creation to perfection through the Logos, now incarnate in Christ, leading to the transformation of this world into the new kingdom. This will bring the return of Christ and the resurrection of the dead who will receive eternity life in the new kingdom upon their belief in Christ.

The question of life after death I also approach from creation. God created humankind as the highest creature in his creation, out of love and in his image. Therefore it is reasonable to assume that God will have humanity share in the perfection of his creation. Our mortality is not a punishment for disobedience, but a necessity for the evolution of life that God chose to bring forth humans. In our sorrow about the loss of a loved one, we may feel consoled in the expectation of meeting each other again during the interim period and thereafter forever in the new kingdom.

The interim period between our death and resurrection is hardly mentioned in the Bible because Jesus and his followers expected the transformation within their life time. I turn therefore to the near-death experiences that cannot be satisfactorily explained as a neurophysiological artefact resulting from cardiac arrest. NDE can therefore be seen as a brief entry of the patient's mind into the realm of the dead. During brain death the mind leaves the body and remains functioning in observing and memorizing but without the ability to communicate. The immortality of the mind (soul) has been an article of belief since the first few centuries after Christ. The 'life review' I see as a self-judgment in which all wrong actions of the past life are seen. Then follows a learning process led by Christ, the 'Light Person' seen in NDE. This is to prepare us for the final judgment on the last day. The effectiveness of the learning process is shown by the fact that years later NDE still exerts a deep influence on the further life of the patient. Since no human being is without sin, I reject the idea of a two-storied realm of the dead. I also reject a purgatory in which our sins are 'burnt off' as this denies the dignity of humans created in the image of God.

The belief in the resurrection of the dead had arisen already before the resurrection of Christ. The resurrection leads to a 'spiritual' body which is united with the mind that has been residing in the realm of the dead. The new body-mind unity then has at its disposal all knowledge and experience acquired during earthly life and through the learning process in the interim period.

The final judgment I like to see again as a self-judgment on the basis of belief in Jesus Christ. Feigning such belief in the heavenly light will be impossible. Those who, even after the learning process during the interim period cannot profess belief in Christ, condemn themselves to eternal existence in the absence of God. Those who during their earthly life did not come to know Christ, will have ample opportunity to get to know him during the learning process in the interim period.

Eternity life is characterized by the absence of evil, death, disease and suffering. I expect plants and animals to be present in the new kingdom in a renewed ecological order. Based on the NDE reports, we may expect to meet relatives and friends and live with them as one united family. There will be no marital relationship and hence no new births. Overpopulation is not to be feared because the earthly limitations of space and time will be lifted and there will be no population increase.

During the transformation Christ will be the executor. The Logos incarnated in him will provide the energy as in the initial creation. The Spirit will insert the new physical laws, as it did once before. After completion of the transformation, Christ will transfer the kingship to the Father.

The apocalyptic events accompanying the transformation can be translated to our time in terms of exhaustion of raw materials, climate crisis, economic crisis with massive unemployment, all caused by human blindness and greed.

Our life here and now should be in the expectation of eternity life in the new kingdom. We are called as a Christian community and as individuals to erect signs of the new kingdom.

# References and notes

## Introduction

1. Sjoerd L. Bonting, *Tussen geloof en ongeloof* [Between Belief and Unbelief], Meinema, Zoetermeer, Netherlands, 2000, Table 20, p. 107.

2. Sjoerd L. Bonting, ref.1, p.118.

3. Pim van Lommel, Consciousness Beyond Life: The Science of the Near-Death Experience, HarperCollins, San Francisco, 2010.

## Chapter 1

1. Gregory Shushan, *Conceptions of the Afterlife in Early Civilizations*, Continuum, New York & London, 2009;

   Guido Derksen c.s., *Geïllustreerde Atlas van het Hiernamaals* [Illustrated Atlas of the Hereafter], Nieuw Amsterdam, Amsterdam, 2010;

   Relevant articles in Wikipedia.com.

2. Jan N. Bremmer, De ziel, reïncarnatie en het hierna-maals in het oude Griekenland [The Soul, Reincarnation and the Hereafter in Ancient Greece], in: Guido Vanheeswijck en Walter Van Herck, eds., *Religie en de dood; Momentopnamen uit de geschiedenis van de westerse omgang met de dood* [Religion and Death; Moments from the History of Western Dealing with Death], Pelckmans/ Klement, Kapellen/Kampen, 2004, pp.21-42.

3. *Het Tibetaanse dodenboek* [The Tibetan Book of the Dead], 7th ed., Ankh-Hermes, Deventer, Netherlands, 1981.

4. The Celtic religion described here should be clear-ly distinguished from Celtic Christianity that de-veloped in Britain and Ireland in the fifth and sixth centuries.

## Chapter 2

1. N.W. Porteus, Soul, in *The Interpreter's Dictionary of the Bible*, vol 4, Abingdon Press, Nashville, 1962, pp.428-429.

2. Dick Swaab, *Wij zijn ons brein: van baarmoeder tot Alzheimer* [We are our brain: from womb to Alzheimer], Contact, Amsterdam, 2010.

3. E. Jacob, Death, in: *The Interpreter's Dictionary of the Bible*, vol.1, Abingdon Press, Nashville, 1962, pp.802-804.

4. T.H. Gaster, Resurrection, in: *The Interpreter's Dictionary of the Bible*, vol.4, Abingdon Press, Nashville, 1962, pp.39-43.

5.  Isidore Epstein, *Judaism, A Historical Presentation*, Penguin Books, Harmondsworth, Middlesex, England, 1975.

## Chapter 3

1.  H.W. Robinson, *The Christian Doctrine of Man*, T&T Clark, Edinburgh, 2nd ed., 1913, pp.4-67.

2.  R.C. Dentan, Mind, in *The Interpreter's Dictionary of the Bible*, vol 3, Abingdon, Nashville, 1962, pp.383-384.

3.  Guido Vanheeswijck en Walter Van Herck, Religie in de schaduw van de dood [Religion in the shadow of death]; in: Guido Vanheeswijck en Walter Van Herck, eds, *Religie en de dood; Momentopnamen uit de geschiedenis van de westerse omgang met de dood* [Religion and Death, Moments from the History of the Western Dealing with Death], Pelckmans/Klement, Kapellen/ Kampen, 2004, pp.7-20.

4.  Guido Derksen c.s., *Geïllustreerde Atlas van het Hiernamaals* [Illustrated Atlas of the Hereafter], Nieuw Amsterdam, Amsterdam, 2010, pp.95-115.

5.  Dante Alighieri, *The Divine Comedy*, English translation of La Divina Commedia by Robert Kirkpatrick, Penguin Classics, London, 2007.

6.  Note: Following the Dutch theologian A.A. van Ruler (1908-1970), I prefer to use the term 'eternity life' rather than the commonly used term 'eternal life'. The latter term is based on our present idea of time but then extended to infinity, which would inevitably seem to lead to boredom. 'Eternity life', on the other hand, indicates living in the eternity of the new kingdom, life that has left transiency behind and knows no limitation of time.

7.  Christa Anbeek, *Overlevingskunst. Leven met de dood van een dierbare* [The Art of Survival. Life after the Death of a Loved One], Ten Have, Kampen, 2010.

## Chapter 4

1.  Wouter J. Hanegraaff, *New Age Religion and Western Culture, Esotericism in the Mirror of Secular Thought,* Brill, Leiden, 1996, pp.270-271.

2.  Sjoerd L. Bonting, *Tussen geloof en ongeloof* [Between Belief and Unbelief], Meinema, Zoetermeer, NL, 2000, p.118.

3.  Pew Forum on Religion & Public Life, *Many Americans Mix Multiple Faiths,* December 2009.

4.  *Geloven in het publieke domein* [Believing in the Public Domain}, Report WRR, ed. W.B.H.J. van de Donk et al., Amsterdam University Press, Amsterdam, 2006.

5.  Michael Tymn, *The Afterlife Revealed: What Happens After We Die*, White Crow Books, Guildford, Surrey, UK, 2011.

6.  Michael Cocks, *Afterlife Teaching from Stephen the Martyr; Conversations about the Spiritual Life*, White Crow Books, Guildford, Surrey, UK, 2011. Previously published as: *The Stephen Experience; Teachings of Stephen the Martyr)*, Kelso Press, Auckland, NZ, 2005.

7.  Guido Derksen et al., *Geïllustreerde Atlas van het Hiernamaals* [Illustrated Atlas of the Hereafter], Nieuw Amsterdam, Amsterdam, 2010.

## Chapter 5

1. Arpad A. Vass, Dust to Dust; The brief, eventful afterlife of a human corpse, *Scientific American*, **303** (3), 38-41, 2010.

2. Robin Marantz Henig, When does life belong to the living?, *Scientific American*, **303** (3), 32-37, 2010.

3. Miranda T. Schram et al, Multimorbiditeit: de nieuwe epidemie [Multimorbidity: The New Epidemic], *Ned. Tijdschrift voor Geneeskunde* **86** (1), 23-25, 2008.

4. Thomas Kirkwood, Why can't we live forever?, *Scientific American*, **303** (3), 24-31, 2010.

5. Frank J. Tipler, *The Physics of Immortality: Modern Cosmology, God and the Resurrection of the Dead*, Doubleday, New York, 1994.

6. Bert Keizer, Vijf stijlen om stervensangst te beheersen [Five styles to control fear of death], *Trouw*, 11 Nov. 2010.

7. Boudewijn Chabot, with Stella Braam, *Uitweg. Een waardig levenseinde in eigen hand* [The way out. A dignified end of life in our own hand], Nijgh & Van Ditmar, 2009.

8. Frits de Lange, De dood is een taboe en moet dat ook blijven [Death is a taboo and should remain so], *Trouw*, 23 April 2011.

## Chapter 6

1. Raymond A. Moody, *Life After Life,* Bantam Books, New York, 1975, 26th printing, 1978.

2. Raymond A. Moody, *Reflections on Life After Life*, Bantam Books, New York, 1978

3. Maurice Rawlings, *Beyond Death's Door*, Sheldon Press, London, 1979.

4. J.C. Hampe, *To Die is Gain: The Experience of One's Own Death*, DLT, London, 1979.

5. Phillip L. Berman, *The Journey Home. What Near-Death Experiences and Mysticism Teach Us About the Gift of Life*, Simon & Schuster, New York, 1996.

6. Peter and Elizabeth Fenwick, *The Truth in the Light, An investigation of over 300 near-death experiences*, Headline, London, 1995.

7. Allan Kellehear, *Experiences Near Death*, OUP, New York, 1996.

8. Mark Fox, *Religion, Spirituality and the Near-Death Experience*, Routledge, London, 2003.

9. Jeffrey Long with Paul Perry, *Evidence of the Afterlife: The Science of Near-Death Experiences*, HarperCollins, New York, 2010.

10. W.C. van Dam, *Doden sterven niet* [The Dead do not Die, Kok, Kampen, 2nd ed, 1980.

11. Pim van Lommel, *Consciousness Beyond Life: The Science of the Near-Death Experience*, HarperCollins, New York, 2010. [English translation of: Eindeloos bewustzijn, Ten Have, Kampen, Netherlands, 14th ed., 2009]

12. P. van Lommel et al, Near Death Experience In Survivors of Cardiac Arrest: Prospective Study in the Netherlands, *The Lancet*, **358**, 2039-2042, 2001.

13. Pim van Lommel, ref.11, pp.135-158.

14. George G. Ritchie, *My Life after Dying*, Hampton Roads, Norfolk, VA, 1991.

15. Pim van Lommel, ref.11, pp.114-134.

16. Hypercapnie verklaart bijna-dood-ervaringen [Hyprcapnia explains near-death experiences], *Nederlands Tijdschrift voor Geneeskunde* **154**, 791, 1 May 2010.

17. Susan Blackmore, *Dying to Live: Science and the Near-Death Experience*, Grafton, London, 1993.

18. Carl Sagan, Broca's Brain: *Reflections on the Romance of Science*. Ballantine Books, 1986.

19. Michael Shermer, Demon-Haunted Brain, *Scientific American* **288** (no.3), 25, 2003.

20. <www.wikipedia.org/A.J.Ayer>

21. Pim van Lommel, ref.11, pp.223-255.

22. Pim van Lommel, ref.11, pp.248-255.

23. Jan Fischer and Daniel Loss, Dealing with Decoherence, *Science* **324**, 1277-1278, 5 June 2009.

24. Stephanie Simmons et al, Entanglement in a solid-state spin ensemble, *Nature* **470**, 69-72, 3 Feb. 2011.

25. Dick Swaab, *Wij zijn ons brein: van baarmoeder tot Alzheimer* (We are Our Brain: From Womb to Alzheimer), Contact, Amsterdam, 2010.

## Chapter 7

1.  W.C. van Dam, *Doden sterven niet* [The dead do not die], Kok, Kampen, Netherlands, 2nd ed., 1980.

2. Klaus Berger, *Is met de dood alles afgelopen?* [Is everything finished with death?], Kok, Kampen, Netherlands, 1998.

3. Pim van Lommel, *Consciousness Beyond Life: The Science of the Near-Death Experience*, HarperCollins, New York, 2010. [English translation of: Eindeloos bewustzijn, Ten Have, Kampen, Netherlands, 14th ed., 2009].

4. Keith Ward, *The Big Questions in Science and Religion*, Templeton Foundation Press, West Conshohocken, Pennsylvania, USA, 2008, pp.160-161.

5. Dinesh D'Souza, *Life after Death, The Evidence*, Regnery Publishing, Washington DC, 2009.

6. Wim Weren, *Dood en dan? Stemmen uit de bijbel, Echo's in onze cultuur* [Dead and Then? Voices from the Bible, Echo's in our Culture], Meinema, Zoetermeer, Netherlands, 2010.

7. Guido Derksen, Martin van Mousch, Jop Mijwaard, *Geïllustreerde Atlas van het Hiernamaals* [Illustrated Atlas of the Hereafter], Nieuw Amsterdam, Amsterdam, Netherlands, 2010.

8. Harmen U. de Vries, *Hoe worden de doden opgewekt? Op zoek naar contouren van het opstandingsbestaan* [How are the dead raised? Searching for the contours of the resurrection existence], Boekencentrum, Zoetermeer, Netherlands, 2011.

9. Pim van Lommel, ref.3, pp.71-72.

10. Klaus Berger, ref.2, pp.153-154.

11. George Ritchie, *My Life after Dying*, Hampton Roads, Norfolk, VA, 1991.

## Chapter 8

1.  Here I made use of the following texts:

    George A. Buttrick, ed., *The Interpreter's Dictionary of the Bible*, 4 vols., 1962, Abingdon Press, Nashville, 1962;

    J.D. Douglas, ed., *New Bible Dictionary*, Inter-Varsity Press, Leicester, England, 3rd ed. 1996;

    Karl Rahner, ed., *Encyclopedia of Theology*, Burns & Oates, London, 1975.

2.  *Joint Declaration on the Doctrine of Justification*, Lutheran Federation and the Roman Catholic Church, 1997, <www.vatican.va/roman_curia/pontifical_councils/chrstuni/documents/rc_pc_chrstuni_doc_31101999_cath-luth-joint-declaration_en.html>

3.  Sjoerd L. Bonting, *Creation and Double Chaos*, Fortress Press, Minneapolis, USA, 2005, pp.94-107.

4.  W.C. van Dam, *Doden sterven niet* [The Dead do not Die], Kok, Kampen, 2nd edition, 1980.

5.  Dinesh D'Souza, *Life after Death, The Evidence*, Regnery Publishing, Washington DC, 2009.

6.  John Baillie, *And the life everlasting*, Oxford University Press, London, 1934.

7.  Karl Rahner, *On the Theology of Death*, Burns & Oates, London, 1961.

8.  Jürgen Moltmann, *Theology of Hope: On the Ground and the Implications of a Christian Eschatology*, SCM Press, London, 1964.

9.  Paul Tillich, *Systematic Theology*, vol. III, Nisbet, London, 1964.

10. Wolfhart Pannenberg, *The Apostles' Creed in the Light of Today's Questions*, SCM Press, London, 1972.

11. H. Berkhof, *Christelijk geloof* [The Christian Faith], Callenbach, Nijkerk, 1973, p.548.

12. John Hick, *Death and Eternal life*, Collins, London, 1976.

13. R. Moody, *Life after Life*, New York, 19th ed. 1977.

14. M. Rawlings, *Beyond Death's Doors*, Nashville, 1978.

15. Klaus Berger, *Is met de dood alles afgelopen?* [Is with the Death Everything Finished?], Kok, Kampen, 1998.

16. Wim Weren, *Dood en dan? Stemmen uit de bijbel, Echo's in onze cultuur* [Death and Then? Voices from the Bible, Echo's in our Culture], Meinema, Zoetermeer, Netherlands, 2010.

17. Guido Derksen, Martin van Mousch, Jop Mijwaard, *Geïllustreerde Atlas van het Hiernamaals* [Illustrated Atlas of the Hereafter], Nieuw Amsterdam, Amsterdam, 2010, pp.205-211.

18. Harmen U. de Vries, *Hoe worden de doden opgewekt? Op zoek naar de contouren van het opstandingsbestaan*, [How are the Dead Raised? Searching for the Contours of the Resurrection Existence], Boekencentrum, Zoetermeer, Netherlands, 2011.

## Chapter 9

1. John Hick, *Death and Eternal life*, Collins, London, 1976, p.273.

2. Klaus Berger, *Is met de dood alles afgelopen?* [Is everything finished with death?], Kok, Kampen, 1998, pp.82-85.

3. *Joint Declaration on the Doctrine of Justification*, Lutheran World Federation and the Roman Catholic Church, 1997, <www.vatican.va/roman_curia/pontif­ical_councils/chrstuni/documents/ rc_pc_chrstuni_ doc_31101999_cath-luth-joint-declaration_ en.html>

4. Sjoerd L. Bonting, *Creation and Double Chaos*, Fortress Press, Minneapolis, 2005, pp.94-107.

5. *The limits to Growth, Report of the Club of Rome*, Dennis Meadows, ed., Universe Books, New York, 1972 (updated version 2004).

# Index

# Paperbacks also available from
# White Crow Books

**All titles available as eBooks, and selected titles available in Hardback and Audiobook formats from www.whitecrowbooks.com**

CPSIA information can be obtained at www.ICGtesting.com
Printed in the USA
LVOW082038280212

270826LV00001B/46/P